Learning and Work

STUDIES IN EDUCATION AND CULTURE
VOLUME 8
GARLAND REFERENCE LIBRARY OF SOCIAL SCIENCE
VOLUME 1069

Studies in Education and Culture

David M. Fetterman, *Series Editor*

Learning and Work
An Exploration in Industrial Ethnography

Charles N. Darrah

Garland Publishing, Inc.
New York and London
1996

Library of Congress Cataloging-in-Publication Data

Darrah, Charles N.
    Learning and work : an exploration in industrial ethnography / Charles
N. Darrah.
       p.   cm. — (Garland reference library of social science ; vol. 1069.
Studies in education and culture ; vol. 8)
    Includes bibliographical references and index.
    ISBN 0-8153-1455-8 (alk. paper)
    1. Occupational training. 2. Employees—Training of. 3. Organiza-
tional learning. 4. Skilled labor. 5. Diversity in the workplace. 6. Educational anthropology.   I. Title. II. Series: Garland reference library of social
science ; v. 1069. III. Series: Garland reference library of social science.
Studies in education and culture ; vol. 8.
HD5715.D37 1996
658.3'124—dc20   95–42416
                                                  CIP

Printed on acid-free, 250-year-life paper
Manufactured in the United States of America

To the Darrah boys:

VINCENT NEIL (1910–1986)
ZACHARY NEIL
JOSHUA ANDREW

CONTENTS

SERIES EDITOR'S FOREWORD

This series of scholarly texts, monographs, and reference works is designed to illuminate and expand our understanding of education. The educational activity each volume examines may be formal or informal. It may function in an exotic and distant culture or right here in our own backyard. In each book, education is at once a reflection and a creator of culture.

One of the most important motifs sounding through the series is the authors' efforts to shed light on educational systems from the insider's viewpoint. The various works are typically grounded in a phenomenological conceptual framework. However, they will vary in their manifestation of this common bond. Some authors explicitly adopt anthropological methods and a cultural interpretation of events and circumstances observed in the field. Others adopt a more generic qualitative approach—mixing methods and methodologies. A few adhere to a traditional phenomenological philosophical orientation.

These books are windows into other lives and other cultures. As we view another culture, we see ourselves more clearly. As we view ourselves, we make the familiar strange and see our own distorted images all the more clearly. We hope this immersion and self-reflection will enhance compassion and understanding at home and abroad. An expression of a common human spirit, this series celebrates our diversity.

David M. Fetterman
Stanford University and California Institute of Integral Studies

PREFACE

This is a book about how we understand work. The topic may seem dry compared to the exotica most anthropologists study, but it is certainly timely. Ruminations about skills, education, and competitiveness fill newspapers, magazines, and books. Even ordinary folks have strong opinions about how best to prepare people for work.

The debate about education and work is strident, and solutions are abundant. Many people feel that education would be more effective if only schools could be more like workplaces. But this raises an important question: What are workplaces really like, and how do people go about their work in them?

Despite bold claims, we know relatively little about this question. Managers often tell us what skills they would like their workers to have, but whether those are the skills needed to succeed at work usually remains unclear. Workers can tell us how they think they perform their daily tasks, but how their explanations correspond to what they do is often unclear. I, for example, have prepared countless lectures over twenty years of teaching, but I cannot fully account for how I do it.

In the pages that follow, we explore how people look at workplaces, and the consequences of those ways of looking for our understanding of work. Along the way the reader will learn something about two manufacturing plants, and much about the minutiae of making wire and cable. These details are necessary precisely because the challenge of working *is* in mastering the details. Hopefully, the lessons learned here can be extended to other workplaces and workers.

Writing a book about work is risky precisely because the topic is so familiar. Most of us are profoundly influenced by our experiences of work, and even before those, by the workers we know. My own case is no different, and I still recall fleeting childhood glimpses of the world of work. I feel that I know my paternal grandfather, although he died years before my birth. A carpenter, he built my grandmother's house and left behind a shelf of carpentry books that I later devoured while curled up on the sofa. My sons live in the same house, and I hope they too will savor those books.

I listened attentively while our machinist friend, Horace Miller, complained to my father that his younger colleagues found it impossible to fashion a cube from a lump of metal using a hand file. He explained that all the machinists of *his* generation could do so. The effect was that of hearing alchemists discuss trade secrets. My father imparted other lessons, those of honesty and reliability, and most of all, about the dignity of just doing your job.

I watched in puzzlement as Harry Borthwick, dressed in suit and tie, wandered along a beach, crouching often to inspect something in the sand. Harry was the scientist of the family, an eminent botanist who opened a boy's eyes to science. Curiosity might have killed the cat, but Harry made a career of it.

Many years and jobs later, I became a landscaping contractor and formed a partnership with Stan Barnes. At first, we discussed everything and shared the arduous tasks of landscaping yards, but gradually we learned what each of us did best. Often we communicated silently, and our movements became a sort of lumbering dance under the hot sun. I was also working as a temporary instructor at a university, when a colleague confronted me about my other life. "Oh, you're one of *those,* a contractor. How *can* you live with yourself," she muttered in disdain. Ironically, I felt that contracting taught me much about honoring commitments, and I feel today that my teaching and research have benefited from my "other life."

A few years later I was a graduate student at Stanford University when I joined a research team that was looking into the relationships among technology, organization, and skills. My proverbial slate, of course, was far from blank. Much of what I had read about work in journals seemed quite irrelevant to my own experiences. Lists of required skills were fine, but they failed to account for the skilled performances I had seen and been part of, and they ignored the settings in which those skills were exercised. This book is an effort to paint a different picture of skills, work, and workplaces.

Like any book, this one is the product of more than my solitary ruminations. Robert Textor, Henry Levin, Richard Scott, and David Fetterman comprised a dissertation committee that allowed me to follow my interests and hunches. The research was part of the Educational Requirements for New Technology and Work Organization Project supported by the Spencer Foundation, and directed by Henry Levin and Russell Rumberger. Michelle

Deatrick, Christine Finnan, Greg Pribyl, and Alison Work were members of the project team and their research helped me clarify my own thinking on work and skills.

Jan English-Lueck, John Garvey, Glynda Hull, Audni Miller-Beach, David Rosen, Andrea Saveri, and Phil Turner provided suggestions and opportunities to develop my arguments. Sage advice was given by James Freeman, my colleague of many years, and the writing of the book was partially supported by a San Jose State University College of Social Sciences Summer Stipend grant. Kathleen MacKenzie's and Lia Boone's assistance permitted me the time to complete the book while getting on with other projects, and Paul McJones provided assistance and solace during several computer crises. Series editor David Fetterman provided the counsel and encouragement that allowed me to see this book through more than the usual crises and interruptions.

The workers of Kramden Computers and Calhoun Wire and Cable were universally helpful and they tolerated my relentless questions with grace. They showed me a world of work far more encouraging than the one often portrayed by prophets of doom.

Finally, my family gave me the opportunity and motivation to undertake this book. It is based on a doctoral dissertation that I completed with the support of my parents, Helen and Vincent Darrah. My wife, Janice Konevich, and boys, Zachary and Joshua, allowed me the indulgence of hours spent writing, and it is to them that I owe the greatest debt.

Charles N. Darrah

Learning and Work

I THE RHETORIC
OF SKILL REQUIREMENTS

Edward, a supervisor at Kramden Computers Company,[1] reclined in his chair and assessed the impact of his firm's newly instituted "team concept" on its production floor:

> Right now we have one spokesperson who has to tape record the meetings and have her daughter translate them each night. That's just insane. The team concept means that workers who just did what you tell them, the kind of worker you *wanted*, won't be enough anymore. We'll need people who can talk and cooperate on their team. And it's too bad, because those other sort of workers built this company.

His words seem ordinary, even commonplace; after all, his lament about the gap between what work requires and what people bring to the workplace is widely echoed. Indeed, Edward's struggling spokesperson provides a vivid, almost comical, case of the worker who lacks a required job skill. Similar tales are recounted by employers across the country as evidence of the obvious: Work is changing and all too many people are ill-prepared for the changes at hand.

Edward's remarks are also unexceptional because they frame the problem in a way that is deeply rooted in the American formulation of common sense. Specifically, the team concept is presented as an inevitable, externally imposed feature of the organizational landscape, one to which workers must adapt by having the correct bundle of skills. Edward's call for a different kind of worker—and the sudden abandonment of another kind who built the company—thus seems to be the logical and responsible managerial response.

Yet Edward's comments leave unsaid much of importance, and their very familiarity reflects deep, tacit assumptions about the world of work and its proper description. Indeed, his remarks suggest a working world that is quite exotic. In this world, change comes from elsewhere and cannot be resisted. Workers are not active participants in the workplace but rather are acted upon by management and other experts. Questions about incentives—for example, to cooperate and talk—are absent, for supervisors are able to demand that workers act appropriately. Just *what* workers will cooperate and talk about is curiously unspecified.

Edward's comments also reveal a privileged perspective on the workplace. He assumes that he sees what is *really* occurring on the production floor, and that he understands its implications for his job and those of his workers. The latter, he believes, are about to experience large changes at work, but the work of supervision will apparently continue as it is. His work will change only if he has to look hard for a different kind of worker.

To recapitulate briefly, Edward's remarks might be ordinary, but they reveal important, unexamined assumptions about power, control, and human agency. They assume an omniscient view of the workplace in which changes in work are predictable and can be described through the neutral discourse of skills.

The purpose of this book is to challenge the view of work just described. I argue that the world of work is far more complex and unpredictable, and that workplaces and work practices are at least as important as skills. Most important, I suggest that the failure to understand this richer view of work distorts the role we give schools in preparing people for work.

We proceed by lingering for a while on Edward's production floor, chatting with his workers, watching them make computers, and observing their engagement with the team concept and a series of ill-fated training classes. Then we pay an extended visit to another company, Calhoun Wire and Cable, in order to trace the outlines of an expanded view of work and workplace. The learning that we encounter there is far more complex, creative, and ambiguous than is typically portrayed in the dire accounts of poorly skilled workers that we routinely encounter.

CRISIS IN THE WORKPLACE

Concerns about education's role in preparing people as workers are not new, but they reached a crescendo in the mid-1980s. Beginning with *A Nation at Risk* (National Commission on Excellence in Education 1983), policy reports, scholarly tomes, and the popular press alike have proclaimed a national crisis in education, thereby fueling calls for reforms such as improved computer literacy, educational restructuring, and national testing.[2] These concerns continued into the 1990s, as evidenced by *What Work Requires of Schools,* the Department of Labor's influential SCANS Report (1991), and the policy concerns of the Clinton administration. Indeed, a virtual cottage industry of future workplace skills reports has emerged.

Although the literature regarding future workplace skills is diverse, the reports collectively paint a picture of the skills required of American workers. Most postulate a set of academic skills, including reading, writing, and mathematics or numeracy, and a set of higher cognitive skills that build upon the first; for example, reasoning, creativity, and critical thinking. The need for workers to be flexible is reflected in the need for problem solving and the ability to "learn to learn." Communication skills, including oral expression and listening, are widely cited, and they merge with and support a diverse set of social skills. Providing feedback, teamwork, and the ability to collaborate in heterogeneous groupings are widely cited. Interpersonal skills, conflict resolution, and negotiating skills are mentioned, as is understanding the operation of the workplace organization. Finally, a heterogeneous set of desirable work habits and attitudes is mentioned (e.g., self-direction, initiative, independence, pride, punctuality, and enthusiasm). Even a cursory review of these skills reveals ambiguities and inconsistencies, but most important for the present argument is that the reports consistently use the concept of *skill requirements* in order to describe work.

The stakes in the current policy debates are especially high since the spread of new technology and forms of work organization are apparently transforming job requirements. Thus, just when schools are accused of failing in their mission to educate, workplaces are demanding workers with more—and different—skills. Further heightening the sense of urgency are demographic shifts in which more new workers will be drawn from historically disadvantaged populations, and the challenges faced by American firms trying to compete in a global marketplace will increase.

This is exceedingly complex public theater, and the plot of the play being performed is convoluted at best. Especially striking is that despite bold claims and strident calls for action, little empirical evidence showing how people actually work makes its way on stage. Perhaps because of the sense of urgency, or because everyone is assumed to be an expert on the subject of work, debate about the "skills gap" has rapidly proceeded from alarms to solutions.

Descriptions of what people do at work would clarify the forgotten, "workplace side" of the skills gap, but instead we have witnessed a rhetoric of skill requirements in which sweeping generalizations are made with apparent certitude. By a "rhetoric of skill requirements" I mean any attempt to analyze work by decomposing jobs or people into constituent characteristics that are somehow necessary for the work to be performed. Precise terms vary, and include abilities, competencies, and capabilities.[3] Although they may be defined somewhat differently, these terms reflect a common view in which jobs or people are decomposed into discrete components that are analyzed and then reassembled. And despite disagreements about the importance of specific skills, there is little question that this is the natural and obvious way to analyze jobs and workers. Despite disagreements about the importance of specific skills, or whether job skills are rising or falling, the concept of skill provides the lingua franca in which the debate is conducted, one that seems too obvious to question.

It is precisely the ease with which business and industry leaders, educators, policy makers, and ordinary citizens describe work in terms of skills that warrants attention. The concept of skill embodies a culturally specific way of looking at workplaces and workers, one consistent with broader features of American worldviews. It is precisely this consistency that makes the resulting accounts of work seem so ordinary, sensible, and realistic. In fact, such accounts are quite exotic, embodying as they do assumptions about how best to understand the world. Work and workplaces are represented as phenomena readily analyzed by outside experts and new workers alike. It follows that gaps in understanding what work requires are largely problems in measurement rather than in the basic conceptualization of work.

A goal of this book is to delineate how the concept of skill requirements molds our thinking about work, and to explore alternate ways of looking at workplaces, ones that may affect the definition of acceptable or reasonable educational responses. It proceeds by presenting extensive case study materials resulting from ten months of ethnographic fieldwork in two manufacturing facilities. Considerable detail is included to illuminate the complexity of even routine, ordinary work in order to present these materials. The purpose of this exercise, however, is to explicate the complexity of understanding work and workplaces, and the implications for educators of settling for the "thin descriptions" (Geertz 1973) that result from analyzing work into bundles of required skills.

This book, then, is as much about the process of observing work as it is about the work itself, and it perhaps reflects my own fragmentary, incomplete, and flawed understanding of the workplaces where I spent many months. While I believe that my understanding has improved, it remains incomplete; what work in these places is "really" about was never revealed through fieldwork. In this sense, the book is intended to serve as a cautionary tale for those who make bold and sweeping generalizations about work based on scanty or nonexistent data.

Despite the certitude of the policy reports, trends in skill requirements are more ambiguous than presented. Although positions are complex, they reflect four arguments about trends in job skills: skill levels are increasing ("upskilling"), decreasing ("deskilling"), contingent on many variables, or being polarized into high and low skill jobs. Proponents of the upgrading thesis argue that aggregate job skills are rising due to the characteristics of new technology that automate routine work, allow workers to focus more on problem solving and improving the production process, and accordingly require that workers understand the larger production systems of which their jobs are only a part. The upskilling thesis is cogently articulated by Blauner (1964), and it emphasizes how technology drives skills upward (Adler 1986; Hirschhorn 1984).

Other theorists argue that skills are being downgraded as jobs are increasingly deskilled through the inexorable logic of capitalism, which seeks to routinize work in order to reduce the cost of labor while simultaneously increasing managerial control of potentially recalcitrant workers. This position is articulated in Braverman's *Labor and Monopoly Capital* (1974), which spawned an extensive debate concerning the labor process in Great Britain and the United States (Form 1987; Thompson 1983), and case studies of specific occupations or industries (Gartman 1986; Noble 1984; Zimbalist 1979). These theorists criticize the technological determinism associated with the upskilling thesis and generally argue that new technology reinforces labor's subordination.

The upskilling and deskilling theses have been predominant, but other perspectives emerged as the flaws of each became apparent during the 1980s. Some theorists began to emphasize the contingent nature of skill requirements as work organization and new technology interact in unforeseen ways. Zuboff (1988), for example, argues that new technology potentially automates work, thereby decreasing job skills, but that it can also be used to free workers to improve the production process, thereby adding value to their work and resulting in higher-skilled, "informated" jobs. Goodman, Griffith, and Fenner (1990), too, argue that similar technologies can be configured in ways that have different impacts upon tasks, making it difficult to predict the skill requirements of individual jobs.

The contingency approach has led researchers to seek to identify the conditions that shape job design (Kelley 1990), such as shopfloor politics that characterize the firm (Wilkinson 1983) or the presence of labor unions (Cornfield 1987). It suggests that skill requirements may be neither simply rising or falling, but rather that the mixture of specific skills required for jobs may be changing. Spenner (1988) and Cyert and Mowery (1989) conclude that there is no compelling evidence for either the massive upgrading or downgrading of skill requirements. They argue that changes in work are best viewed as requiring a *reskilling* of the work force. A related interpretation is that skill requirements are polarizing, with some jobs being upskilled while others are routinized and deskilled.

These perspectives on skill requirements have implications for educators. The upskilling thesis implies that the demand for more able workers is increasing, and it has been used to rationalize widespread educational reforms leading to increased basic skills, familiarity with computers, and national educational standards. The deskilling thesis, of course, suggests quite the contrary. The implications of the emerging contingency perspective are predictably less clear, but in general support the importance of the basic skills that increase a worker's capacity to understand and adapt to changing circumstances, as well as the social skills that allow new forms of work organization to function. The polarization perspective is perhaps most challenging, for it suggests that there is little justification for a national effort to upgrade skills, although it may be in the interest of any individual to do so.

Further discussion of the skilling debate is beyond the scope of this book, but it is significant for the present argument that its participants express changes in the nature of work in the idiom of skills and skill requirements. Thus, there appears to be a consensus among educational policy analysts, academic theorists, and political commentators regarding the usefulness of the concept of skill for expressing complex changes in the nature of work.

The skill concept may be ubiquitous in discussions of work, but its use is inconsistent and often ambiguous. Skill levels are sometimes inferred by reference to broad occupational groupings, or they may be indirectly measured by reference to wage rates or educational levels. Alternatively, skills may be directly measured by various survey, archival, or historical methods (Spenner 1990). Vallas (1990) identifies three categories of studies of skills. National aggregate studies, such as the *Dictionary of Occupational Titles* or "DOT" (U.S. Department of Labor 1977), utilize aggregate data in order to infer skill levels and their educational implications (Spenner 1979, 1983). Restricted quantitative studies follow a similar strategy in assessing skills but do so in specific industries or regions. Studies of the printing industry conducted by Wallace and Kalleberg (1982) and of clerical work by Vallas (1988) represent this approach. Finally, a variety of qualitative studies assess changes in skills within firms or occupations. For example, Noble (1984) traces the impacts of automatic machining tools on the skills of machinists, while Kraft describes the evolution of computer programming (1979). Both authors describe a process of deskilling, as jobs are simplified through a combination of changes in production technology and the organization of work. Hirschhorn (1984) and Zuboff (1988) describe the impact of information-based technologies on skills, and they generally emphasize their potential for creating "upskilled" jobs.

Collectively, these studies paint a broad picture of skills in the United States, although it is one open to conflicting interpretations. In general, the national aggregate studies support the upskilling view of work, although conclusions based on them must be approached with caution (Spenner 1990). The restricted quantitative and qualitative case studies are heterogeneous, and their results are more difficult to interpret. The labor process debate has produced case studies which (predictably) document the deskilling of jobs (Zimbalist 1979), although other studies have documented the limitations faced by management as it seeks to impose control in the workplace and to deskill jobs (Wilkinson 1983; Halle 1984). Other case studies have presented evidence of upskilling (Attewell 1987).

Despite a vast and heterogeneous literature, relatively few studies of skills are based on direct observations of people at work or on interviews with workers. Instead, conclusions about changes in skills are generally inferred from formal job descriptions that ignore the exigencies of life in specific workplaces and the practical expertise developed by ordinary workers (Halle 1984; Kusterer 1978). Indeed, it is this practical expertise that is critical for understanding work, but that is seldom captured by formal descriptions of work (Baba 1991). While studies of skilling may reveal gross skill levels, they do not provide sufficient resolution in order to assess how actual workers perform their jobs. Thus, they provide an inadequate basis for any but the most general claims about appropriate educational responses.

Studies also differ in where they situate skills. Skills may be conceptualized as characteristics brought by individuals to the workplace, an approach favored by psychologists emphasizing human abilities (Fleishman 1975) and economists such as Becker (1975) who conceptualize skills as human capital. Alternatively, job analysts and sociologists typically treat skills as characteristics of jobs or tasks, independently of the people who perform them. It is this conceptualization that underlies the labor process debate and, ironically, the current calls to better prepare workers for more skilled jobs. The DOT, for example, rates occupations on dozens of characteristics which have been used to construct measures of the complexity of the worker's interactions with people, data, and things. Despite extensive criticisms (Spenner 1990), the DOT remains the most comprehensive classification of occupations available, and is widely used by sociologists of work.

More recently, the SCANS Reports, such as *Skills and Tasks for Jobs,* decompose skills into five categories of competencies that are "skills necessary for success in the workplace," and "foundations," or skills that underlie them (U.S. Department of Labor 1992, 1–3). These skills were classified and defined by a group of experts prior to analysis of any actual jobs. The importance of each skill for fifty different jobs was then determined by interviewing three to five persons who either performed or supervised each job. SCANS reports a high degree of consistency among the job raters, although the report cautions against applying the results to jobs in particular organizations. Various approaches to job analysis (Hackman and Oldham 1980; McCormick 1979) and performance appraisal (Gruenfeld 1981; Henderson 1980) also conceptualize skills as attributes of jobs or tasks, as does the DACUM method of job analysis that is widely used in vocational education (Norton 1985).

SKILL REQUIREMENTS AS WORLDVIEW

This brief review of the skilling literature suggests that it is a large and diverse one. Likewise, the concepts of skill and skill requirements are diverse, reflecting a variety of purposes and disciplinary perspectives. Nevertheless, the ideas that task and role requirements constrain the actions of workers and that human contributions can be conceptualized as discrete skills seem intuitively correct to most observers. The assumption that task and role requirements and the abilities of workers must somehow correspond is too obvious to question.

Although the notion of skill requirements appears plausible, it implies an observer who, following some explicit or implicit operations, labels some skills as necessary in order for the work to be performed. Yet discussion of these often concealed observers, and the assumptions and understandings they bring to their role, is typically omitted. This is a significant omission, for labeling skills as required reflects the interests and power of different people within the workplace. That the identification of required skills is not merely a technical operation is demonstrated by feminist studies of work (Cockburn 1985), sociological studies of the construction of occupations and professions (Collins 1979), research into the question of comparable worth of jobs (Reskin and Roos 1990), and studies of the labor process (Braverman 1974; Zimbalist 1979).

Conceptual frameworks of skill requirements entail assumptions about the self and others, environment, causality, and the organization of space and time (Kearney 1984). When we use such concepts we are not simply describing a world awaiting discovery, but rather descriptively providing worlds with particular contours and features. The concept of skill requirements is accordingly selective, pointing us in some directions while diverting us from others. The result may be analyses of work that are consistent with the worldviews of the analysts, but that are only tangentially related to how people work. Educational strategies predicated upon these enacted worldviews might be satisfying to those who employ them, but they will be inadequate in other important ways.

Four tenets of the concept of skill requirements are germane to educational reform.[4] The first tenet decomposes workers or jobs into bundles of attributes (i.e., skills), thereby reducing them to discrete components. These skills are typically defined a priori, as in the case of the SCANS Reports, thereby facilitating comparison among different jobs or occupations. These skills are in principle mutually exclusive, and collectively they form a complete and exhaustive description of the job or the worker. The result is an idealized worker who is assumed to use a particular profile of skills, although no actual worker need do so.

A second tenet is that the skills identified are required in an obvious way, and the implication is that if they were lacking the work would not get done. This suggests that workers holding identical jobs or performing the same work must be in command of the same skills. There is an individualism operating here: The proper unit of analysis is the individual job, and individual incumbents must in principle be identically skilled. All this implies a clarity and certainty of what is needed in order to perform on the job, and a sense that the relative importance of skills is obvious and can easily be assessed. There is also a tacit, normative quality to skill requirements, for they reflect how, according to someone, work should be completed.

The clarity of skill requirements is significant since it is the basis for tests designed to assess a prospective employee's potential to perform on the job, the assumption being that such tests are valid indicators of how effective workers perform their tasks. A corollary is that evidence for the assumed gap between job requirements and worker abilities may be based on failure rates on employment examinations, not on evidence of failure on the job.

Third, the concept of skill requirements isolates workers and jobs from the larger context in which they are embedded,[5] and it treats particular workplaces as the backdrops behind skilled performances. In the extreme, the skilled worker is one who moves freely between backdrops, carrying his or her skills like so much luggage and then transferring those skills effortlessly into new workplaces.

The specific contours of context are seemingly inevitable, shaped by exogenous and inexorable factors with universal effects, such as technological innovation or market competition. These effects constrain the tasks that must be completed and, accordingly, the skills required to do so. In effect, these external changes call for a worker who has been designed to meet specifications or "basic skill requirements." The authors of *Workplace Basics*, for example, argue that technological change, innovation, and increasing marketplace competition are upskilling work (Carnevale, Gainer, and Meltzer 1988, ii). Driving this change is an effort by firms to reduce the cycle time between innovation and production, thereby providing them with a competitive advantage. As employees become involved in this effort, skills are affected by

> movement toward more participative management and employers aggressively driving workers toward decision-making at the point of production or point of sale, and it is easy to see that new skills must be applied if employees—and their employers—are to succeed in the marketplace. (Carnevale, Gainer, and Meltzer 1988, iii)

The underlying model of skill requirements is clear: "Changing economic and technological realities alter the institutional structures themselves. And these new structures, in turn, change basic skill requirements" (Carnevale, Gainer, and Meltzer 1988, 4). Thus, skills and workplaces are transformed by external forces that cannot be altered by workers or managers. The best response becomes adaptation to the inevitable.

The fourth and final tenet is that workplaces and the actions that occur in them are phenomena amenable to study by the methods of positivist science. Specifically, skills are conceptualized as irreducible elements of people or jobs, analysis of which is based on a rather uncomplicated process of description. Resulting accounts of workplaces are clear and unambiguous, and although the descriptions of observers might differ if they witness different events, these would only serve to clarify the description and not to fundamentally transform it. For example, a longer period of observation should result in a more detailed description, but it should not result in a radically different understanding of work.

In this view, problems in analyzing work are largely problems in measurement, not the conceptualization of work; the latter can be taken for granted. That analyses of skills and skill requirements may result from political agendas, or that they may reflect the normative visions of individuals and groups is unacknowledged. Description is straightforward, and skills provide a neutral metric in which to express the salient features of the workplace.

It is this tenet that makes possible unambiguous lists of the skills required to perform in the workplace. From this perspective, learning in the workplace consists largely of internalizing the preexisting knowledge and developing the predefined skills; there is little room for creativity in this model of learning. Problems in workplace training thus consist of technical difficulties in transferring information from those who possess it to those who do not. This provides an official curriculum for the new worker who will be formally and informally tested as to his or her mastery of the correct lessons.

It is the central argument of this book that these tenets profoundly simplify our understanding of work, and by doing so they constrain the actions we believe will result in improved workplaces. Specifically, the tenets draw our attention in two diametrically opposed directions. On the one hand, they lead us to focus on the irreducible characteristics of workers who effectively become bundles of requisite skills. How such a bundle is integrated into the worker's identity and life is extraneous in such an analysis. On the other hand, we are led to look to macroscopic processes, such as global competition, technological innovation, and demographic trends, in order to understand the environment in which skilled performances are constructed. Thus, specific workplaces become irrelevant for understanding work. The positivist stance only reinforces the assumption that there are unambiguous requirements to which individual workers must conform.

ORGANIZATION OF THE BOOK

The remainder of this book explores the adequacy of the concept of skill requirements as the obvious, universal model of work. The concepts of skill and skill requirements are deeply embedded in both expert and everyday understandings of work, and they are clearly useful for many purposes; relegating them to the intellectual scrapyard is not a goal of this book. What is being challenged is their adequacy as the basis for understanding how people actually perform work in actual workplaces. Better understanding of the latter, in turn, is necessary for any attempt by educators to improve the capacity of people to work effectively.

Chapter 2 provides an initial excursion into one workplace. We visit Kramden Computers, a manufacturer of computer workstations, which had recently organized its production workers into teams, and we follow the company's attempt to provide training in order to reduce problems in workmanship. The saga of Kramden Computers allows us to assess the adequacy of the concept of skill requirements for understanding the ultimate failure of the training program.

Chapter 3 reviews the literature on practical reasoning, situated cognition, activity theory, and practice theory that provides a basis for an alternative view of work. This view informed the ethnographic fieldwork conducted in a second site, Calhoun Wire and Cable Company, the description of which constitutes the remainder of the book.

Chapter 4 explores the naive realism of viewing workplaces as natural objects that observers can easily describe. It explores how both workers and the ethnographer described the workplace in ways that made sense, but in fact simplified and distorted the complexity of work.

Chapter 5 presents extensive descriptions of the practices related to running machines in order to "make product," the basic task of an operator. These practices are related to the properties of specific machines, the patterns of feedback that characterize the production floor, and organizational expectations.

Chapter 6 extends the discussion by exploring how perceived changes in competition have resulted in increased paperwork, meetings, and projects that have in turn altered production floor practices.

Chapter 7 analyzes how the production floor is structured as a community of practitioners, how newcomers enter it, and how the community shapes the learning that occurs there. We pay special attention to the production-floor worldview, and how operators are enculturated into it.

Chapter 8 analyzes several trends that are affecting production work and the worldview. We explore these by describing how a new cabling machine and an automated production control system are affecting work. The chapter concludes with a cautionary note about the tensions that characterize the production floor and make it difficult to precisely predict future job skills.

Finally, in Chapter 9 we make a brief visit to NewSite, Calhoun's "factory of the future," in order to glimpse how changes in the workplace have affected production work. We conclude with a discussion of the characteristics that seem to affect learning in the workplaces we have explored.

I want you to tell them what they need to know in order to build better systems.

—Dean, the production manager,
speaking to a group of engineers

They know how they think they are built, or they know how they should be built, but they don't know how they are actually built.
—Dean, speaking about the engineers a week earlier

FIRST EXCURSION

We begin our assessment of the concept of skill requirements by exploring the production floor of Kramden Computers, a northern California manufacturer of multi-user computers. Our focus is on a training class developed by the company in order to reduce the ubiquitous "workmanship problems" that plagued the production floor.[1]

The training class is especially useful for exploring work at Kramden Computers. Its design and implementation reflected the assumptions of the production manager, supervisors, and various engineers about the nature of the production process; the responsibilities of different categories of workers; and the nature of the workplace and learning within it. While production workers had their own ideas about the same topics, managers, supervisors, and engineers were able to define problems and enact solutions to them. The training class can thus be viewed as an arena in which assumptions about work and workplaces were given voice, thereby allowing us to make an assessment of the concept of skill requirements. Specifically, we will explore how the training class failed to meet its objective of providing requisite skills and knowledge to the production workers because of an inadequate conceptualization of their work.

Kramden Computers was studied as part of a larger research project designed to assess the impacts of new technology and work organization on skills and, ultimately, the educational policy implications of those impacts.[2] Fieldwork was undertaken in order to assess the difficulty in studying work in real-world settings, and it focused initially on the tasks workers performed and the skills they needed. This fieldwork, as well as that conducted simultaneously at Calhoun Wire and Cable Company, lasted for ten months and provided the basis for several subsequent shorter studies of other workplaces.[3]

The fieldwork involved participant observation among production workers, supervisors, and engineers, as well as extensive interviews conducted with production management. Observations were made of workers while they assembled, tested, or repaired computers. The account of production work presented here is best viewed as an effort that began by looking for skills, although the latter gradually receded into the background as the technology and work organization that shaped the performances of workers emerged.

KRAMDEN COMPUTERS

Kramden Computers designs and manufactures half a dozen model lines of multi-user computer systems for various business applications. Corporate management is organized into four levels (president, vice presidents, managers or directors, and supervisors) administering departments clustered loosely into functional areas. Fieldwork was conducted in the Manufacturing area's production floor. A production manager is responsible for the three departments that comprise "the floor." Below him are two Board Test Department supervisors (one per shift), two day-shift supervisors (one each for the Mechanical Assembly and System Test departments), and one swing-shift supervisor directly responsible for the entire production floor.

Production work consists of assembling a variety of parts into a computer or "system." A system must pass several electronic tests and then successfully load the operating system software that controls its operation. Each system must contain the correct number and combination of modules, such as hard disk, streaming tape, or floppy diskette drives and printed circuit boards (PCBs), each updated with the latest revisions in circuitry and components. Each module has to be properly fitted ("pinned") with tiny jumper cables to make it compatible with the other modules in the system, and a record of its test history and the parts it contains is created (a "paper trail"). Finally, the system is examined by Quality Assurance (QA) inspectors for internal and external cleanliness.

Production workers are assigned to one of three departments. Board Test technicians ("board techs"), who hold electronics technician certificates from community colleges or trade schools, test individual PCBs on automatic test equipment, diagnose ("troubleshoot") PCBs that fail tests, repair PCBs by removing and installing components (e.g., memory chips, capacitors, microprocessors, etc.), and "rework" boards requiring changes in wiring and/or components so as to comply with the latest engineering specifications. Mechanical Assembly assemblers take the parts comprising a unit from delivery carts, install them in a metal chassis, and make the requisite mechanical and electrical connections between parts with screws, cables, terminators, and connectors. The test operators of System Test perform two basic functions. Some test systems by ensuring that diagnostic tests are correctly performed on each system. Other test operators, informally called "repair techs," diagnose and repair systems that fail a test by searching for loose connections, manually running diagnostic tests to isolate the cause of failure, and, if required, installing replacement modules.

Production work is performed by teams comprised of members from each of the three departments. Each team is responsible for one or more models each month. This "team concept" was introduced soon after the field-work commenced, and the production workers remained unclear about their new roles, since previously they had worked only with members of their assigned departments.

Because of its lilliputian size in an industry of giants, the firm invested little in sophisticated production technology. Although its products incorporate state-of-the-art components, they are manually assembled on one of five roller-assembly lines. Electric screwdrivers are the only power tools used in assembly, and pliers, sidecutters, and screwdrivers are scattered on the workbenches. More prominent are the various computer terminals used to test and record data about each computer as it is built. Although this technology gives the workplace a "high-tech" appearance, it is subject to numerous operational problems and variances.

The company has a minimal human resources function, and individual managers are responsible for hiring their employees, most of whom are expected to have requisite experience or certification. Hiring is done through a temporary employment agency, usually on a thirty-day renewable contract, during which time the employee is observed and evaluated. Permanent positions are usually filled by well-regarded temporary workers. Because of the local availability of qualified workers and the presence of alternative employers, attachment to the firm is low and movement between companies is fluid. Kramden Computer's management follows a policy of minimal staffing and is reluctant to hire until a crisis is reached. Annual layoffs are typical, if seldom severe, and are used to remove unwanted employees. Perceived productivity rather than seniority determines who is laid off, and few ex-employees return to the company.

Supervisors complete biannual employee assessments that nominally review performance and recommend corrective actions to improve work skills, but workers failing to act on such recommendations are seldom penalized. Supervisors report that reviews are actually based on attendance and tardiness, both of which are easier to monitor than performance. Although satisfactory reviews support regular pay raises, promotions and lateral moves into other departments are based on a worker's reputation among supervisors, members of the hiring department, and other people who can observe work habits and ability.

Production workers typically learn to perform their jobs through on-the-job training. Formal instruction is minimal since management assumes that new workers possess the requisite skills. A new assembler might work next to a more experienced one for as little as fifteen minutes, learning to imitate the actions of the other as she secures hard-drive modules in their protective cases with a few screws. The trainer soon departs to undertake other work, while the newcomer continues to assemble the remaining drives until they are completed or she is assigned other tasks.

Test operator training has been similar. A veteran worker commenting on his early days in the firm remarked: "There was no real training. I was just exposed to five tests, and not told anything. I just wanted to quit." Board techs are trained through gradual exposure to increasingly complex PCBs. A lead technician explained that he assigns new workers to the automatic testing machines for a few weeks so they learn the characteristics of the individual tests, their sequence, and typical error messages. Then he allows them to troubleshoot simpler PCBs, such as memory or input-output boards. After three or four months, technicians are able to recognize error messages and pinpoint the defective areas of the boards. Gradually, they tackle the more complex PCBs.

For production workers, training has consisted largely of making the best of opportunities to observe the actions of others. Because training is imitative and trainers are uncertified, poor practices can spread quickly across the production floor. There is little discussion of how tasks fit together, how to obtain information, how decisions are made, or how the production floor itself is organized. Formal training has not been valued by the firm, and workers who take the initiative in preparing instructional aids for their co-workers find their efforts unrewarded.

Production management also pursues a strategy of, as one supervisor remarked, "control through ignorance." Workers are discouraged from obtaining the engineering drawings that are formally available to all employees. Schematic drawings are explicitly banned since the supervisors believe that their presence on an assembly line indicates that workers are undertaking repairs beyond their competence. Workers are told only what managers think is necessary for them to do their jobs, and they are uninformed about the functioning of the automated testing system or the various databases.

Learning in the workplace has thus been problematical to management. Managers are torn between the need to inform workers so they can act effectively and the desire to limit unwanted actions by restricting information. Because workers move easily between companies, managers fear that the benefits of training will be taken to other firms. Dean, the production manager, commented that his ability to control labor costs was critical, and he wished to avoid enhancing a worker's value to the firm. This, however, placed him in conflict with engineers, who hoped to see qualified workers formally certified as trainers.

Work and the Training Class

Discussions began in December 1987 among the supervisors, an engineer, and Dean to develop a training class. The goal, according to Dean, was to reduce the workmanship problems caused by the production workers' lack of skills and knowledge. An initial, week-long training class was to be developed for one team, after which the training would be revised and offered to the other teams. Dean articulated the philosophy underlying the classes as one of transferring expert knowledge, and he told the trainers, "I want you to tell them what they need to know in order to build better systems." The production workers were never advised as to the plans for the class, much less asked about their training needs.

The classes finally began in April 1988, with each two-hour class devoted to one or more topics. Monday was divided between an orientation to Kramden Computers and safety on the production floor. Tuesday covered mechanical assembly, with an emphasis on the correct use of engineering documentation. Wednesday was devoted to using the diagnostic tests, and Thursday consisted of a presentation by a Quality Assurance inspector. The course ended on Friday with a one-hour discussion of Production Control, followed by an open question-and-answer session with all the trainers present. The presentations proceeded with little coordination between them, and often consisted of a mixture of orientation to the trainer's department, promulgation of specific procedures, techniques for problem solving, and scolding.

The team members generally sat attentively listening to the trainers present their materials, and began asking questions only after several days of classes. Subsequent evaluation of the classes revealed that most trainees were unclear about what questions could be asked, and others feared that questions would be interpreted as evidence of ignorance.

Asking questions as a component of training became especially contentious. Dean proclaimed, "The class is to be total discussion in which you're encouraged to interrupt at any time. We want you to ask a lot of questions. We want to find out what we have to teach to make everyone good." The trainees confided that the reliance on questions was disingenuous because neither management nor engineers had asked their opinions before, and they claimed it was evidence that the trainers did not know how to teach. More ominously, several senior workers commented that the team would be held responsible if the training failed because they had not asked the correct questions.

There were very few questions about how a particular task should be performed, and instead workers, often responding to the prompting of the trainers, began to ask questions about workplace technology and organization. Soon, they began to use the classes to expand their understanding of production work rather than to obtain information to better perform narrowly defined tasks.

Viewed as activities intended to provide workers with the knowledge and skills to build computers, the classes were unsuccessful. The issue was less whether the workers could assimilate the trainers' prescriptive knowledge than whether that knowledge was relevant to how they necessarily built computers in an uncertain environment under great time pressure with inadequate information, tools, and equipment. It is to this topic that we now turn.

The company's computer assemblers faced ubiquitous shortages of parts, requiring them to reallocate their labor frequently. Although the assembly line ideally presented a smooth, lineal flow of product, a worker might be forced to return to the same units repeatedly over a few hours or days as needed parts arrived. Workers concurred that the tasks of assembly work per se were relatively simple and routine, but they claimed that those tasks did not fully capture the nature of their work. One commented, "remembering where you are" in assembling the computers could be overwhelming, and workers occasionally forgot to complete some assembly steps due to the repeated interruptions. Many units were subsequently rejected at Quality Assurance inspections, a condition the workers attributed to the interruptions.

Repair technicians, too, worked on several defective systems simultaneously. Their work entailed using automated tests to locate faulty parts, "swapping" them for new ones, and then retesting the units. Engineers and managers claimed the work was relatively simple because diagnosing the cause of failure within a module was unnecessary and in fact prohibited. Although workers generally agreed with that assessment, they explained that it missed the point: The challenge was to systematically juggle swapping parts in several units, while awaiting the automated tests to cycle through their sequence.

During one eight-hour shift, for example, I watched while a veteran system repair technician worked simultaneously on six computers, swapping modules between them in order to efficiently localize their faults. When the shift ended he walked to the cafeteria, where he sat quietly alone for thirty minutes, explaining that he usually unwound with a cigarette before going home.

The actual complexity of production work was, of course, suggested by the prevalence of workmanship problems, even among experienced workers. Ironically, production work was presented during the classes as simultaneously simple and complex. An engineer, demonstrating how to position cable clamps within a computer, remarked, "These are positioned by a template designed to make it easier so you don't have to think." Work here was presented as very standardized and routine; not to think was virtuous. But then the engineer discussed how assessing corrosion of the chassis involved considerable interpretation: "It's not self-evident, but what counts as corrosion varies when QA rejects units with markings it may have previously passed." He admonished workers to "look carefully" and "think" before using a suspect chassis. Mechanical assemblers claimed that their work was in fact more complex than recognized by management, and several assembler-trainees demonstrated privately that they could position the cable clamps more rapidly and as accurately without the engineer's template. After all, they did so dozens of times a day.

The trainers presented a view of production work that defined it as a process largely independent of human action. A product engineer's admonishment was typical: "If we build it to the paperwork, it will work." Another engineer conducted his class around building a system using the specified manufacturing assembly drawings, product tree, parts matrix, and bill of material, but workers told him that if they proceeded so systematically they would never meet production quotas.

The team's mechanical assemblers also pointed out inaccuracies in documents, including inconsistencies, incorrect values, and inaccurate drawings. In fact, "building to the documentation" was impossible. The documentation methodically described how each model should be assembled, tested, and inspected, but it failed to specify how (or even whether) workers and technology interacted to do so. Production as an activity conducted by workers was conspicuously missing, replaced by a view of production as a disembodied process.

Some trainers extended their admonitions to individual relationships. One urged team members, "Put pressure on one another to pin the [hard] drives correctly, and if someone seems to have difficulty doing it right, look over that person's shoulder when they pin drives." Team members listened quietly, but confided that such scrutiny was supervisory work, and they were not sufficiently paid to pressure each other. Likewise, the team members demurred privately when another engineer told them, "You should tell each other things you find out," commenting that this was an unwanted intrusion into interpersonal relations.

Trainers consistently asked for information that would help their departments, but that would not directly benefit the production workers. An engineer, for example, exhorted them to "learn part number language" and to master documentation so they could pinpoint problems and advise the engineers. But the realities of production work militated against both extensive cooperation and mastering documentation, as the case of a poorly designed cable suggested. Jerry, a product engineer, was demonstrating the correct way to assemble a new model computer when he began to struggle with the flat cable that connected the halves of the computer. Several assemblers commented that the cable was several inches too long, a problem they had told him about. The cable could easily be crimped, but fitting it in place often resulted in pinched and cut finger tips for the assemblers. Jerry acknowledged their warning but explained that it had taken the form of a crude sketch without part numbers, and thus his response was delayed. "Learn the part number language," he again urged. Then he noted that the company had bought thousands of the questionable cables and could not return them; the team's feedback was thus irrelevant. Privately, workers complained that there were no incentives to learn "part number language" or to alert engineers to problems, because they were usually told that nothing could be done.

A breakthrough of sorts occurred on the fourth day of training. Anh, a Test Diagnostics engineer, was providing an overview of the specific diagnostic tests that were controlled by "Autotest" when he momentarily paused and pointed to a diagram, remarking, "I can't remember which order I put these in." He quickly moved on, but a repair tech interrupted and asked him to clarify "putting the tests in order." Anh explained that he programmed Autotest to control the sequence of diagnostic tests, and the team members looked at each other with surprise. "We didn't know *anyone* did that. You mean you can change the order of tests?" Anh laughed and replied, "Of course. We're always adding or updating tests. Or debugging them."

The repair techs then explained that some models frequently failed the hard-drive test after nearly thirty minutes of testing. The repair tech then had to troubleshoot the failed system and reconnect it to Autotest, which began the testing cycle anew. This wasted time since the system had already passed the earlier diagnostic tests, and so the repair techs asked if the hard-drive test could be moved forward in the sequence.

Anh commented that he was unaware of the problem; the repair techs smiled and nodded as he plotted out a new test sequence. He also explained that he could show them how to perform the test manually to speed up the retesting, but they explained that they needed the Autotest printout as verification of a complete test cycle.

Further inquiries of this sort followed and, in fact, the team later confirmed that this exchange had been most illuminating. One remarked, "How many other things like this are there that we don't know?," and they decided to find out as much as they could by querying the trainers, who were only too willing to provide information. They were annoyed that such information had been concealed, and they identified several members of support departments who could be relied upon to assist them in the future. Several of these trainers, some of whom had reputations as being notoriously unhelpful, were later seen huddled with knots of workers on the production floor discussing problems.

The trainers, too, learned that they did not fully understand the realities of production work as they listened to the team describe the daily problems they had encountered, and as they later consulted with workers among the assembly lines. Anh, for example, said he was surprised that the repair techs did not simply run the tests manually, for he had ignored the production floor reality of creating a "paper trail" for each system built.

Reactions to the training were lukewarm. The workers appreciated the opportunity to acquire information normally not available to them, as well as the chance to communicate directly with engineers and other trainers, but they concurred that the training was superficial and not responsive to their needs. Subsequent conversations indicated that few team members believed they had learned how to perform their tasks better, or how to perform tasks with which they were unfamiliar. Many were insistent in demonstrating to me that they performed their tasks better than the trainers, and several demonstrated how they had creatively and secretly solved several recalcitrant problems that had confounded the engineers.

Workmanship problems persisted as the company continued to reduce its permanent workforce due to a slump in sales. Dean promised further training classes after the traditional summer shutdown, but his critics grew in number and he became a victim of the summer layoff. The training classes were discontinued.

SKILL REQUIREMENTS REVISITED

We turn now to the question of how the concept of skill requirements fares in analyzing production work in Kramden Computers. First, everyone (including the ethnographer) conceptualized the problem that training was to be addressed in terms of the skills needed to perform specific tasks. Thus, we all spoke the rhetoric of skill requirements, thereby reifying it as the obvious, natural, and correct way to describe work. However, the discussions of work that occurred during the class were embedded in much larger worldviews characteristic of different departments and occupations. Class discussions were as much about explicating and negotiating these worldviews as about determining the skills required to build a computer.

We begin with the failure of the formal curriculum to deliver the skills needed to assemble computers correctly. Dean and the supervisors desired virtually algorithmic procedures, but these were not forthcoming. Many of the trainers' prescriptions were rebutted by the realities of production work, and the various omissions and inconsistencies in the prescriptive model served to remind participants that it was impossible to "build to the documentation." The ambiguous definition of training, in which it merges with developing procedures, also suggests that the prescriptive model must be clearly developed before workers can be trained to follow it.

If the prescriptive model was not developed, the current reality was not understood. Even Dean confided that no one clearly understood how computers were being built: "They know how they think they are built, or they know how they should be built, but they don't know how they are actually built." The various trainers individually revealed their ignorance of many current practices, so that the training classes unintentionally established that Kramden Computers knew neither how it built computers nor how it should build them. Narrowing the gap between the actual and the ideal was therefore logically impossible.

A resolution to this dilemma would have been to orient the training classes around discovering how computers were built, the results of various practices, and ways to allow the production workers and management to work with other departments to improve the production process, but this alternative was never considered. To do so would have changed the role of production workers as learners, the value of their knowledge, and the very definitions of learning and work. The foundations of "control by ignorance," too, would be eroded. "Control of the process" defined the core responsibility of a manufacturing engineer, and accordingly production workers were excluded from discussing it and told instead to improve their workmanship, that is, to flawlessly perform the transformations specified in "the process."

Resolving this dilemma would also have required confronting several deep-seated principles of corporate life. Departments were without formal charters specifying their responsibilities. These were established by tradition in the industry and through a demonstrated willingness to solve problems in the firm. Kramden Computer's employees, while enjoying the absence of rigid charters, complained of being overburdened with problem solving, and most avoided at least some problems by defining them as the responsibility of other departments. Several engineers, for example, commented that they avoided "seeing" some problems in order to increase their control over their own schedules.

Ironically, the absence of charters was intended to provide organizational flexibility, but it had contributed to creating an organization in which departments seldom worked to develop common solutions to problems. The common sentiment was that if each department would do its job, then Kramden Computers would prosper; accordingly, the causes of systemic problems affecting several departments were rarely addressed. To engage in the organizational learning that would improve production would have violated not only norms regarding the hierarchical relationships between engineering and production work, but also broader corporate norms governing how departments functioned and careers advanced. Thus, not only did the training curriculum prove untenable, but alternative formal curricula were unthinkable because they breached established norms concerning the organization of work.

The specific tenets of the concept of skill requirements are also challenged by the reality of work in Kramden Computers. We begin with the assumption that work can be fully analyzed by decomposing jobs and their incumbents into constituent skills. Work in Kramden Computers suggests three challenges to this tenet. First, much of the discussion of needed workplace skills emphasizes the new, presumably higher-order skills that are required when new technology or participatory forms of work organization are introduced. Yet one very traditional feature of work figures prominently in accounts of work by Kramden's production workers: Workers simultaneously perform multiple tasks. Workers frequently noted the expectation of gracefully handling tasks thrust upon them suddenly. While production supervisors called this skill "flexibility," team members complained that it minimized the value of planning, another valued skill. It also reduced worker opportunities to demonstrate initiative since they spent considerable time managing an imposed workload.

Workers often explained that while their isolated individual tasks were manageable, in actuality they performed many of them simultaneously, and it is that burden which posed the challenge. This contrasts markedly with the engineer's view of production work, in which skills can be inferred from the methodical assembly of computers. It suggests that while work can surely be decomposed into skills, something very important may be left out: the temporal dimension of tasks and their overlapping nature. How the worker actually manages this complexity is typically omitted, since the job is described as a timeless set of tasks, not a shifting interdependent flow of activities. Incorporating this aspect of work into our analysis, however, steers us away from individual tasks and workers, and instead directs us to how work is organized in the workplace.

A second challenge to the tenet of decomposability can be seen in the response of workers to the team concept. Management, engineers, and production workers alike conceptualized the challenge this presented in terms of the correspondence between the skills they believed it entailed and the skills they believed production workers possessed. For example, engineers speculated as to whether the workers had the communication skills to conduct the two or three brief team meetings each day. The team concept, however, had implications for workers as people, and not merely as bundles of skills.

The situation was similar to that seen in companies in which managers attempt to achieve control via "strong corporate cultures" (Deal and Kennedy 1982; Peters and Waterman 1982). Hochschild (1983) and Kunda (1992) note that such strategies seek to internalize corporate values and norms in workers by manipulating public rituals and symbols. Regardless of their ultimate success as a managerial tool, these strategies are associated with "deep acting" (Kunda 1992, 156) by workers who are compelled to present convincing performances as particular kinds of people as bases for continued employment. What the worker feels ceases to be private, and workers may eventually become the people that they initially only pretended to be. Working in such workplaces may well require interpretive and presentational skills, but it requires much more as well—the engagement of the whole person.

The team concept entailed changes not only in skills, but in worker identities as well. Workers were advised that each team was to act as a separate company, with the members thinking of themselves as its "vice presidents," a claim that most workers said was cynical considering the company's historical denigration of their abilities. Likewise, they were admonished to monitor and correct each other, thereby altering existing definitions of the person and his or her relations with others. In one dramatic episode, two members of one team developed an intense dislike for each other that resulted in repeated screaming matches on the production floor, a source of amusement to other teams and acute embarrassment to the team's "spokesperson." The latter felt obligated to mediate the dispute "for the sake of the team" and to protect his own reputation as a leader, but he was essentially powerless to rebuke his coworkers.

The Vietnamese workers, who comprised about 40 percent of the workforce, were especially fearful of the team concept, which they likened to communist work teams. One supervisor's explanation that each team's diverse members were to work together "at the same level" only exacerbated their belief that communism had indeed followed them to the United States.

The team concept as implemented thus altered existing relationships among workers who believed that they were insufficiently compensated to mediate disputes, despite the pressure to do so. Workers argued that the team concept forced them to embrace the fortunes of the firm, something they resisted doing due to their own lack of job security. Yet most felt compelled to act as if they enthusiastically embraced the team concept in order to demonstrate their willingness to cooperate and be "team players." Thus, they engaged in the sort of deep acting postulated by Hochschild, which not only altered the discrete skills they needed to perform effectively but also impinged upon their individual identities as workers.

The decomposability tenet is also challenged by the manner in which skills were socially constructed in the workplace. The ability to "see the big picture," so desired by production management, is a prime example. We examine this skill because of its similarity to the "systems competency" identified in the SCANS report; other reports mention comparable skills.[4] Identifying this capability as a skill situates it in jobs or persons, and thereby allows observers to hold the worker responsible for seeing or not seeing "the system." Yet whether workers see the big picture is also a function of what there is to see, the access workers have to it, and their incentives to look.

Seeing the big picture on the production floor takes the form of work teams planning their daily production of computers. This involves taking a monthly production target and computing the number of units to be built each day to reach it. The task is complicated by the fact that the computers pass through automated tests that can take several days to complete, so more computers must be assembled early in the month in order to have sufficient "product in the pipeline" as the end of the month approaches. The teams resisted both taking the daily inventory of "their" computers as well as performing the calculations needed to determine the next day's "build total."

Supervisors lamented the inability of teams to regulate their daily production of computers, but the workers argued quite differently. From their perspective, learning to understand the entire manufacturing process and to perform the calculations to determine a daily production target are irrelevant. Production of PCBs is subcontracted to several vendors and shortages of needed parts is a daily occurrence that is beyond their control. Why, they asked, should they waste time on calculations that are rendered superfluous when a vendor fails to deliver PCBs as promised? Likewise, reconfiguring boxed computers to meet customer demand or to implement changes specified by engineering renders careful planning irrelevant. And, they argued, if they meet production targets, management simply brings out more "kits" of parts to assemble: There is little incentive to meet production targets.

Workers also complained that management adopted a very self-serving definition of the big picture. One group of workers, for example, had requested and been granted a tour of the Customer Service Department in an adjacent building. Because workers in that department perform many of the same tasks as the production workers, they were seeking ideas about performing their work more efficiently, and seeing firsthand what sort of faults afflicted the products that were returned. Although this visit was reportedly useful to everyone involved, the production manager banned further trips because he feared his workers might use them to transfer to another department.

This wider historical context of production floor relations must be considered when we assess claims about the importance of seeing the big picture. In Kramden Computers, there are tacit limits that workers have to discover, for clearly they are not encouraged to inquire about everything, regardless of management's statements. Again, we see the importance of being able to interpret the often implicit constraints that guide curious workers as they explore further and further away from their assigned tasks. Thus, the systems that production workers are meant to see are not lying there awaiting discovery, but they are often concealed by the same supervisors and managers who lament their workers' inability to detect them.

These three challenges to the adequacy of the concept of skill suggest that what we observe when we study a workplace is produced by a system shaped by technology and organization, as well as the more obvious actions of workers. From this perspective, what we see people doing at work represents only a manifestation of this larger system of relationships, and we cannot fully comprehend the former without explicating the latter. This also suggests that the concept of skill may function to blame workers for breakdowns in much larger workplace systems. In this sense, the concept of skill is value-laden in that it directs our attention to the actions of workers, but not to the historically conditioned relations within which they work.

The notion that skills are required in some obvious way is also challenged by the fieldwork. Skill requirements rest upon the idea that some skills are more critical or important in order to perform tasks. Although this idea is intuitively plausible, the fieldwork demonstrated that importance itself is problematical. Sometimes importance refers to a judgment that some skills are central to a job. Mechanical assemblers, for instance, necessarily exhibit fine motor coordination in order to position and secure computer components in a chassis. Skills important in this sense must be exercised in order for a task to be completed.

Importance often refers to the level of a competency required by a worker. Competence in problem solving fits this pattern. It is infrequently used by many workers, but when it is needed it is perceived to be needed at a high level. Less competent workers still work effectively because there are relatively few instances when the competency is required. Skills may also be deemed important if they are used constantly, even if at a low level; oral communication among team members fits this pattern.

Skills assume importance in two other ways. Sometimes a skill is an important factor in being hired for the job, although it is relatively unimportant for job performance. Kramden's management, for example, borrows standard job descriptions from other local firms, a widespread industry practice. As a result, system repair technicians are required to understand specific electronic principles such as Ohm's Law, although they, the engineers, and the production manager stated that these principles are irrelevant to the job.

Alternatively, a skill can be important for career advancement. Oral communication is displayed constantly on the production floor, albeit at low levels of proficiency. However, it is an essential skill in order to build a network of helpers from other departments and to establish a reputation as a desirable worker. Thus, the team concept stimulates supervisors to seek out production workers with better communication skills, although those skills are actually more important in obtaining and later leaving the job than they are in working as a team member.

The notion of skill requirements also assumes that incumbents of the same job confront a common set of tasks and employ identical ways of completing them. However, the fieldwork indicated alternative ways of performing tasks that may entail different skills. *This suggests that a set of objective characteristics of tasks need not require a single set of skills.* For example, "troubleshooting" PCBs is the central task of Board Test technicians, and the latter explained it as an exercise in logical deduction. In fact, the technicians employ a variety of strategies in troubleshooting, and nominally identical workers develop different repertoires of strategies. While logical deduction and the ability to trace circuitry on schematic diagrams is important, their use is time-consuming and the company restricts to one hour the time a technician troubleshoots a single PCB. Accordingly, technicians rely extensively on their memories of the causes of similar failures, and most proceed by trial and error to narrow the search for the fault. Some technicians reportedly "play" with faulty PCBs when their own logic and memory fail, and all routinely consult with other technicians regarding recalcitrant failures. This suggests that tasks, even if required of a job, may not determine a single set of skills needed to perform them.

The fieldwork also indicates that the sense in which a skill is required, too, can be unclear. On the one hand, workers often fail to do things at work that are in some sense required of the job, although they remain valued employees. For example, written communication skills are needed to compose unambiguous memos between the day- and swing-shift halves of each team, but few if any workers possess them. Miscommunication is endemic, and feuds between workers on different shifts can suddenly erupt and persist for days. Management desires improved written communication skills, the lack of which has clear costs in the workplace; thus, the skills are somehow required. Still, the sense in which a competency is required becomes problematical if it is missing among virtually all workers.

Other required skills are even more problematical since they reflect inefficiencies in the workplace. The plight of system repair techs who repair systems by swapping potentially defective modules for new ones is another example. The formal procedure for such swapping involves completing a form, taking the module to a window, and receiving a replacement for it. Due to parts shortages, the delay in obtaining a replacement can take hours, thereby lowering productivity. The techs also suspect that the parts they return may be returned to stock, only to see them reappear days later in new kits of parts. With the tacit approval of their supervisors, these techs have developed strategies to manipulate paperwork in order to maintain hidden caches of spare parts to avoid trips to return them. Mastery of these strategies is required in order to maintain productivity, but the reorganization of the parts-swapping system in order to eliminate its inefficiencies is clearly another option.

The lesson to be drawn from these examples is that skill requirements are not derived in any simple way from asking people about their jobs (or the jobs of others) or observing them at work. Skill requirements are constructed through a social process, and we may legitimately ask how that construction proceeds.

The third tenet, that skills can be fruitfully isolated from the context within which they are exercised, is also challenged by life on the production floor. The company builds products from industry-standard components; it holds no patents. Its competitive advantage results from quickly developing products that efficiently utilize technological breakthroughs pioneered by other firms. It is subject to intense market pressures, and has weathered repeated cycles of layoffs and hirings. Manufacturing has low status within the corporation since it has never been linked by management to any competitive advantage. As we have seen, training production workers is not a high priority, although products are typically rushed to market before being fully tested and cannot be assembled by referring to preexisting procedures. Managers do not see the paradox of denigrating production work as "basically simple" while simultaneously complaining about workmanship problems that, after all, imply an absence of the skills the workers are not supposed to need.

Different departments within Kramden Computers affect work on the production floor. For example, the company builds its products for independent distributors who delay purchases as they shop for bargains. Only one-quarter of the monthly production total is known at the start of a month, making it difficult to plan more than five days ahead. The delays in orders are exacerbated by the distributors who are on a calendar month rather than the fiscal month used by Kramden. Since the latter ends about the twentieth of each month, the distributors have another ten days before the end of their month to place orders, so they attempt to delay ordering just when Kramden's salesmen pressure them to do so. The Production Control Department attempts to anticipate demand, but production workers are constantly removing completed units from the warehouse and "reconfiguring" them for last-minute orders. The lack of a linear production flow also results in ubiquitous parts shortages, such that as one worker noted, "We always are starting to build one thing, and winding up with something else." He and other workers complained that the constant interruptions contributed to the workmanship problems.

The Design Engineering Department decision to build computers from modules installed in a chassis and secured with a few screws and connected by cables also shapes tasks and skills. These modules are fabricated by external vendors and shipped to the production floor, thereby limiting the variety of tasks performed by workers. Such modules are miracles of technological complexity, but workers are prohibited from penetrating their workings.

Modular components and subcontracting-for-assembly services create surfaces that make inner workings invisible and lessen the opportunities to explore and learn more than rudimentary assembly, testing, and repair skills. They also indirectly affect the opportunities and incentives to give and receive feedback that could effect changes in both manufacturing processes and product, since vendors are often far removed or parts may be purchased in large quantities.

Although this case reveals the importance of the workplace in shaping actions, it is not a functional whole that molds skills in consistent directions. The production workers encounter contradictions in their experiences that have to be managed, even if they cannot be resolved. For example, while the team members were told to be vice presidents of their own teams, they noticed that management retained all its former prerogatives. Workers were unable to allocate their team's labor to perform even trivial tasks, such as labeling bins of hardware—when they tried, supervisors told them to "get back to work." They were encouraged to cooperate freely on their team and to compete vigorously with other teams. Management in fact anticipated that the team concept would provide productivity gains due to both increased cooperation and competition. However, knowing *when* cooperation and competition are appropriate can be confusing. In one dramatic incident, a team refused to loan a system repair technician to another team, arguing that they needed her expertise at the time. A supervisor decisively and permanently removed the system repair technician from the team. When news of the event spread rapidly, teams immediately began quietly removing themselves from choice opportunities.

Team members pointed out the contradictions between the behavior expected of them and the behavior exhibited by management. They commented that they were asked to communicate openly, while management operated in secrecy. They argued that the cooperation they were asked to demonstrate was not rewarded in the company, for they saw uncooperative people routinely promoted. They heard others boast of "getting" or "beating up" people in other departments through various stratagems, and concluded that cooperation was not rewarded in this firm. Still, they performed as if they were committed team members who communicated openly and cooperated with others.

Finally, our exploration of production work suggests that describing and learning about work is more complex than assumed by the concept of skill requirements. As we have seen, the production floor is diversely skilled and much work is unrecognized by management and engineers; there is no monolithic set of foundational skills, and the actions of individuals blur with characteristics of the workplace. Describing work, designating tasks as necessary, and inferring required skills are all seen to be normative endeavors that reflect the understandings of different people as to what work is and should be. Descriptions of the workplace are thus partial and incomplete, and always taken from a perspective that limits what can be attended to. There is no comprehensive, foundational description of the workplace—only tacit, fragmentary ones that periodically surface during events such as the training classes.

The diverse understandings of work are extraordinarily complex, reflecting assumptions about the self, its relations with other people, hierarchy, knowledge, and causation. The power to enact or reify understandings of the workplace is differentially distributed; after all, management and engineers were able to define the production workers as the problem needing solution. Accordingly, the description of skills is embedded in contests for organizational power, and it is not the dispassionate, neutral analysis of requirements typical of the future workplace skills literature.

The internalization of knowledge, too, provides an inadequate conceptualization of learning in the workplace. Comprehensive knowledge about how computers were actually built was unavailable, as was strikingly revealed during the training class. Although production workers had much to learn from the engineers, the latter also had significant gaps in their knowledge of computer assembly. Learning, however, was constrained by the organization in ways that made improving both productivity rates and product quality difficult to achieve. Kramden's production worker trainees were defined as ignorant and unskilled, so their knowledge was seldom solicited. Exploration of how computers were in fact built was not undertaken because to do so entailed a degree of collaboration that violated departmental boundaries and occupational hierarchies. And learning was defined as something that occurred in special settings, far removed from work on the production floor. In fact, the workplace itself provided a curriculum that was more persuasive than the formal lessons of reluctant trainers.

In conclusion, our exploration of Kramden Computer's production floor suggests that while the concept of skill requirements can be used to describe work, it does so by performing an enormous simplification to our understanding of it. This, in turn, has implications for how we think about people at work, as well as how best to prepare those people for jobs that we incompletely comprehend. The argument is not that the capabilities of people at work are irrelevant, but that how we think about the relationship of people to workplaces is inadequate in important ways. Developing an alternative way to understand work is the topic to which we now turn.

3   SKILLS, CONTEXT, AND PRACTICE

We want you to think of yourselves as vice presidents of your own company. Each team is a company.

—Dean, announcing the team concept
to the production workers

So we just took her and moved her to the team.

—Alan, a supervisor, commenting
on removing a PCB tech from her assigned team

You mean you just moved her from her team temporarily, until those boards were done?

—Author

No, I mean we moved her fucking permanently! They're not grasping how to use members on that team.

—Alan

In the last chapter we explored the failure of the concept of skill requirements to explain work in a setting where work is routinized and, according to some of Kramden's supervisors, even unskilled. In this chapter we develop the idea that Kramden Computer's production floor constitutes an arena that constrains the learning within it. Any workplace can be viewed as such an arena for learning, one that may teach lessons quite different from those intended by the bearers of official lessons.

ARENAS OF LEARNING

Learning is not a single, homogeneous activity on the production floor, but rather it is complexly structured and viewed differently by several categories of people. Accordingly, we can identify how the workplace structures the individual and the collective learning that occurs there. We begin by discussing the two instructional activities recognized as such by management: on-the-job training and the training class. The former is poorly developed, but it is how workers traditionally learn to perform their jobs. Next, we revisit the training class that constituted Kramden's attempt to provide more rigorous and formalized instruction. We discuss both the formal goals for the class and the different ways its participants conceptualized the activities appropriate to it.

Kramden's on-the-job training and the training class differed in important ways, but both were acknowledged by everyone involved as deliberate efforts at instruction. Other learning is not so intentional, and in fact it is not recognized as such by management, engineers, or workers. Here we will explore the lessons learned through the daily experiences of workers as they assemble, test, and repair computer systems and PCBs. Thus, quite apart from the formal attempts to provide instruction, experiences are structured by the organization of work and the technology used, and those experiences provide a powerful, largely unacknowledged curriculum.

In order to analyze on-the-job training and the training class we adapt and build upon Goodnow's (1980) model of popular theories of instruction. Cultures differ in their construction of instruction as an appropriate activity, and theories of instruction may be compared along several dimensions. First, a theory of instruction entails general assumptions about the nature of knowledge, what is valuable within the culture, and what can be taught. Second, it is based on assumptions about learning as a bounded activity. Where teaching and learning should occur, and how teaching is demarcated from other culturally constructed activities is one aspect of bounding. Broad metaphors about teaching and learning that typically draw upon wider cultural meanings may be identified. Activities thought to permit learning such as telling, showing, doing, and watching may also vary. Stages of learning and an individual's progress between them may also be defined. Third, theories of instruction imply roles such as instructor and student, which are parceled out among different people. Who should teach, who should learn, and the responsibilities, incentives, and penalties associated with each role are critical. The patterns of discourse and social interaction appropriate to teaching and learning can also be distinguished.

Learning on the Job: Informal Instruction

Instruction on the production floor traditionally takes the form of a poorly developed system of on-the-job training. Knowledge is viewed as a commodity that can be transferred from one person to another. Like a commodity, it brings power to those who possess it, and it may be reduced in value by sharing. Accordingly, knowledge is a medium for barter among workers, and it is the currency used to build informal networks of coworkers.

The process of knowledge transfer is accomplished by newcomers listening to the statements of other workers assigned to instruct them in performing some task. Instructors also provide opportunities for learners to observe exemplary performances. Knowledge is task-based and related directly to the labor of assembling, testing, and repairing PCBs or computer systems. Knowledge about the nature of the production floor as a work organization, the functions of supporting individuals and departments, or the nature of interpersonal relationships on teams is conspicuously absent, it being assumed that workers will "pick it up" as needed.

Knowledge is located in several places. Written documentation, largely produced by various engineering departments, specifies critical parameters of both the products and the processes used in constructing them. However, much of this knowledge is unclear to workers who are unable to interpret the often complex diagrams or instructions, which are directed primarily to other engineers. Training in the use of documentation is nonexistent, and work areas are littered with binders of unused documentation. The aforementioned practice of "control by ignorance" and the rapidly changing engineering documentation limit the usefulness of such sources, and knowledge about building computers is largely orally transmitted. Knowledge is also demonstrated in the performances of exemplary workers and can thus be learned if the newcomer is sufficiently observant.

Knowledge is also organized by occupations or job titles, so that there is knowledge associated with assemblers, test operators, repair techs, and board test technicians. In fact, each job title is defined both by the tasks its workers are assigned and by the knowledge thought to underlie effective performance of those tasks. This organization of knowledge is critical for understanding the tensions within work teams. High-status and more educated workers, such as board test technicians, worried that lower-status workers would learn how they performed their work, a situation they deemed unfair since the latter had not "earned" that knowledge by attending a local community college or trade school. Conditioned to be at the pinnacle of the production floor hierarchy, they expressed dismay at being compelled to perform lower-skilled assembly or system testing work.

For their part, workers in lower-status jobs feared being evaluated on their ability to perform tasks for which they were unprepared. They understood the reluctance of any worker, regardless of status, to share the knowledge which allowed them to maintain their positions, and they especially doubted their power to force higher-status workers to provide adequate explanations or even opportunities to observe skilled performances.

The occupational structuring of knowledge is also affected by the attachment of workers to firms and industry-standard occupational definitions. The latter allows Kramden Computers to hire production workers with predictable skills, and these new workers generally assume that their tenure with any firm will likely be brief. Accordingly, developing greater knowledge in the occupation or in anticipation of a career advancement is eagerly pursued, and many workers attend electronics courses in a local community college. But cross-training in divergent skills only produces workers with skills valued by Kramden Computers, an investment workers said had a low payoff.

It is widely believed that effective instruction occurs in settings where work occurs. Classrooms are suspect and associated with abstract, theoretical knowledge of marginal relevance to the ultimate test of knowledge: improving yields on the production floor. Among assemblers, instructors describe and demonstrate a task, and then depart to perform their own work. System repair techs and board technician instructors usually permit novices to work nearby for extended periods of time, generally giving them simpler tasks to perform until they gain mastery, but even here learning is not allowed to interfere with meeting production quotas. On-the-job learning is thus serious business that is embedded in production work, and any attempts at playfulness or experimentation are prohibited.

In all areas, instruction is predominantly oral, and knowledge is stored in the memories of workers rather than in formally approved engineering documentation or in notebooks maintained by workers. In fact, the latter are explicitly prohibited since the information they contain has not passed through a formal engineering review process. Despite this, most assemblers keep notes with diagrams of the correct pinning of modules and the combinations of modules that comprise particular models of computers in order to avoid searching through lengthy engineering documents.

As we have seen, production work has been historically devalued by the firm and training is deemed a luxury. Production work is "real work" according to supervisors and teaching is not conceptualized as requiring any special preparation. Good instructors are not formally rewarded nor are their production assignments reduced. Alternatively, there are no penalties associated with poor teaching. Effectively fulfilling the role of instructor does, however, confer some benefit. Instructors can demonstrate patience, commitment to improving the firm, and verbal skills that can enhance reputations and can subsequently be converted into a promotion or lateral move off the production floor.

Because teaching is devalued and unstandardized, there is great variability in instruction. For example, several assembler-trainers were observed directing a novice to a pile of parts, demonstrating once how to put them together, and then rapidly departing to perform other tasks. Their only words of instruction were "Put them together and tell me when you're done." Other trainers create hierarchies of assembly tasks and carefully explain the reason for each operation. Although instructors are expected to have mastered the tasks they teach, there is no systematic attempt to verify their knowledge or their ability to teach it to others. This allows current information to be quickly transmitted, but it also promulgates the spread of rumor and misinformation.

For newly hired workers, on-the-job training is associated with a probationary period during which they are most vulnerable. And because hiring is done only under pressure, more experienced workers have scant time to offer assistance; instead, they focus on increasing their team's production. Learners are expected to be attentive so that instructions need not be repeated. While they are free to ask questions about *how* a particular task is performed in Kramden Computers, they are expected to avoid asking *why* it is performed. Likewise, questions should ideally focus on tasks and not the larger organization of the workplace. Learners demonstrate proficiency by quickly replicating the skills they have received by maintaining expected levels of productivity; there are no assessments or examinations. Trainers recognize no differences among learners, and simply offer their standard instruction to each student.

Some on-the-job training actually takes the form of self-instruction. Several workers, for example, called themselves "scroungers." They had worked widely in the industry and could, as one commented, "find out anything I need by asking around." Or, both types of system test operators served at least limited apprenticeships if they were fortunate, but several learned their jobs by borrowing the owner's manuals shipped with the systems and reading them at home or at their work stations.

In summary, instruction is viewed as a necessary evil, one which could be eliminated if workers arrived bearing adequate knowledge of their jobs. From the perspectives of management and engineers, the purpose of on-the-job training is to replicate an extant production system, and learning by production workers is not linked to improving that system. Workers, on the other hand, value training that enhances their career opportunities and they argue that the failure to provide it reflects Kramden's lack of commitment to them.

The training class represented a singular instructional event, one intended by engineers and management to constitute a paradigm for future instruction. Knowledge to be imparted during the classes consisted of unambiguous series of operations that produced acceptable, identical products. Such knowledge was produced by experts, here in engineering or other supporting departments, who have the right and responsibility to impart the correct algorithms to others.

The ultimate source of knowledge was "the process" controlled by Kramden's engineers. It defined a series of step-like operations that must be performed on specified materials, although it did not specify whether these operations were performed by machinery or people. Human action on the production floor was thus abstracted from the process which seemingly built systems.

The knowledge to be conveyed through training was generated by an elite certified to define, maintain, and transmit it, and who could alter it only by following formal rules for doing so. The production process was conceived as a linear one, and the knowledge that defined it was exhaustive: It was all that was really necessary to know in order to build computers.

Training knowledge was abstracted from the actual operations performed on the production floor. While it specified the operations providing the instructor with his (all instructors were male) authority, it failed to specify the human actions even in principle, how those actions become coordinated, or how people interacted to carry them out.

The crux of the failure of training was the gap between the actions taken by production workers to build computers and the process that incompletely defined how they should be built. Worker actions were based on knowledge, but as we have seen, that knowledge was illegitimate according to the instructors. The knowledge of the latter was legitimate, but disembodied and removed from the actions necessary to build computers. This gap between real and ideal could have been the focus of mutual efforts to learn, but status differences supported by industry-wide occupational definitions mitigated against recognizing the gap, much less bridging it.

The knowledge valued in the process concerned direct labor in assembling, testing, and troubleshooting computer components using extant technology and operations. There were, however, a few peripheral attempts to specify algorithms for conducting interpersonal interactions such as cautioning a teammate to follow procedures. These were ignored by the trainees. Likewise, algorithms for organizational processes were both imparted and subverted, as exemplified by management's exhortations to "get around" the cumbersome procedures of other departments.

Algorithmic knowledge was transferred to learners in a setting removed from production work. Normal rules of interaction were suspended within this setting: The questions of learners were requested or even demanded. In fact, learners were responsible for asking questions that demonstrated interest and intelligence. These provided continuity throughout the presentation in the absence of a training needs assessment conducted on the production floor. Management viewed asking questions as unproblematic, although they claimed that many Indochinese workers were afraid to reveal their ignorance in the presence of coworkers and thus might decline to ask the questions that were on their minds.

From the perspective of the learner, the questioning format was doubly threatening. Despite management's exhortation to ask questions, they feared their supervisors would interpret this as indicative of ignorance and would later seek retribution. In addition, they claimed that any failure of the training class would be attributed to their failure to provide abundant "good" questions. In fact, instructors were responsible for the accuracy of the algorithms they presented, but not for providing an effective instructional design. The emphasis on questioning was especially ironic since it would necessarily vanish in the planned videotaped training.

Instruction consisted of describing algorithms or demonstrating them via paradigmatic performances. The ability to comprehend and follow algorithms was partially a function of the learner's existing knowledge, although the latter was not assessed prior to training. Learners were thus conceptualized as identical. The results of training were to be assessed by pre- and post-training comparisons of a team's yields at various test and inspection stations, although these were never implemented. Whether algorithmic knowledge was successfully transmitted or acted upon was never to be assessed.

In summary, the training class was marked by several contests which appeared anomalous from a strictly instrumental view of training. Learners and instructors differed in their interpretation of questioning. The latter saw questioning as unproblematic; after all, they were successful at it. The learners, however, felt it could be used to punish them and was being solicited only because the instructors were so ill-prepared. Questioning required an initiative by the learners that implied both a commitment to the firm and an acknowledgment of the superiority of the instructors' knowledge, neither of which the learners were prepared to make.

A related contest was joined over the authority and relevance of the algorithms. Learners silently watched as engineers instructed them in tasks that they had long since mastered. They tried tactfully to explain the reality of production floor work and the strategies they used to meet production deadlines. Thus, a sort of guerrilla warfare was conducted over the legitimacy of the knowledge possessed by learners and instructors, as well as the power of one group to compel another to pay attention to its concerns.

A third contest took place over the conflicting interests in learning how to perform valued and devalued work, with higher-status workers feeling they were being robbed of hard-earned skills while they were demeaned by being forced to learn low-status assembly work. This was a contest over who should pay attention to whom, as much as what they should do on the job.

Because the training class failed to perform its instrumental function of transferring algorithms to learners, it soon devolved into an arena in which all parties tried to explore that which was normally taboo and to establish claims on other departments. Training was especially suitable for this precisely because of its cultural construction as a safe setting for exploration, but the final result was still to blame workers for their failure to learn properly.

We see then from our exploration of instruction in Kramden Computers that, despite the bounding of instruction, the latter was always embedded in task performance, interpersonal interactions, social constructions of proper skills, and the historical relationships among different categories of workers. Learning via instruction of any sort thus always occurred in a larger context in which workers learned from the exigencies of production-floor life, and it is to that topic that we now turn.

The Production Floor as an Arena for Learning

Thus far we have discussed intentional efforts at instruction on the production floor, and in both cases found them to be deeply embedded in production work. We now turn to the workplace as an arena in which learning occurs independently of instructors, curricula, or formal settings for learning. Here we examine the production floor as an arena that structures the experiences of workers in ways that convey lessons at least as powerful as those imparted by formal instruction.

First, despite instruction directed at individual learners, work is completed within complex social networks. Control by ignorance and obtuse engineering documentation results in the need to mobilize assistants to interpret information and decode it into more accessible forms, such as sketches of correct hard-drive pinnings for specific models. However, such drawings are illicit and possession of them is forbidden. The relative lack of useful written documentation is reflected in the binders of seldom used paperwork stashed next to each team's assembly line, and in the oral tradition that transmitted knowledge to build computers. Attending to stories and comments, and having access to at least a few helpful assistants are critical for success on the production floor.

Several aspects of the social nature of Kramden's production work stand out and shape the learning which occurs there. The necessity for social networks is unacknowledged by management and so the ability to construct such networks is devalued by supervisors. Workers who try to build and maintain such networks are often admonished to get back to work, and some develop reputations as laggards. Furthermore, many of the tasks undertaken within production floor networks are illicit and expose the workers involved to rebuke.

Second, the workplace can be analyzed as a set of surfaces that block gaze in some directions and direct it in others. This structuring of attention shapes learning in profound, often unrecognized ways. Subcontracting and the use of modular components eliminate opportunities to enter sealed units and explore inner workings. The absence of rights to view most kinds of documentation and to ask questions of engineers also creates barriers to learning. Supervisors define tasks and restrict workers to knowing only that which they judge necessary to complete them. Many facets of workplace life remain opaque to workers. Although several computerized testing systems are central to their work, they were unaware of how they functioned or who controlled them. Likewise, they were barred from knowing how production targets are determined each month or, more generally, how other departments function within the company.

Third, appearances are suspect. This was exemplified by the suspicion with which workers greeted the arrival of the team concept in a workplace that had historically denigrated worker knowledge, but other technological and organizational examples abound. Fluctuations in the local electric grid cause irregular, "flaky" failures in the computer systems being tested. The resulting error messages can send system repair techs on futile searches for causes. The company purchased several different brands of "loopbacks," electrical connectors plugged to the data ports of computers, while they are tested. These varied in quality and defective ones can cause the computer to fail a test. When the test operator removes the loopbacks (according to procedure) and sends the faulty computer to a repair tech, the new loopbacks installed by the latter can produce a different error message, or none at all. In addition, there are errors in engineering documentation and in the testing messages, which lead workers to distrust what they see. For example, due to a programming error, a "failed test message" actually means a "passed test message" on one test.

More generally, the relationship between failure messages and corrective actions is loose. The same failure message is often caused by different defective parts, and likewise, identical defective parts can cause different failure messages. Further complicating matters, information technologies sometimes serve unintended functions. A system designed to assist repair techs in diagnosing failures is occasionally used by management to monitor productivity by calculating the monthly number of repairs each tech performs.

Fourth, there are constraints upon the ability to take action within larger systems of learning that link the detection of problems with the outcomes of problem solving. This was vividly demonstrated when teams participated in a Closed Loop Corrective Action Program intended to identify problems encountered during production. Responsibility for resolving each problem was then allocated during a weekly meeting of manufacturing managers and supervisors. Although production supervisors were initially skeptical, the teams immediately identified scores of problems that were then assigned to other manufacturing areas. The very success of the program was its undoing: The other areas argued that they had insufficient resources to redress the problems and the program was soon terminated. Workers commented that this reflected their general plight: If they made mistakes they were immediately blamed by other departments, but they could not comment on the errors of the latter.

Other attempts to amplify worker learning have been rebuffed. Board test technicians, for example, want to immediately take the PCBs they diagnose to a "rework station" where the specified repairs are actually performed, and then to retest them to determine if their diagnosis is correct. This, they have argued, will enhance their capability to learn from experience. However, management insists that the demand for PCBs on the production floor should drive the allocation of the repair technician's labor, and so all diagnosed PCBs are placed in a queue and repaired hours or days later. This effectively bars the technicians from knowing conclusively the results of their troubleshooting efforts. No compromise has been developed, so technicians illicitly beg and cajole the rework technician to work on especially recalcitrant PCBs out of sequence.

Fifth, the workplace is essentially produced by people external to it, supervisors, engineers, and the support staff. It is a set of stage props designed elsewhere, but one that constrains the actions of production workers. Attempts to work *on* the workplace by suggesting designs for equipment or work procedures are barred. For example, the layout of the assembly lines and the organization of work stations was changed according to management's design; the ideas of workers were not solicited. Even the training class was kept secret from the teams, and a training needs assessment was not conducted. Work is direct labor performed on products, and never the production of the workplace itself. Accordingly, we speak of the tasks performed in the workplace but never those performed on the workplace, for the latter are exclusively the province of management.

In summary, production workers learn that different categories of people in the workplace have different perspectives on learning and work, and these perspectives are embedded in differential power. They are compelled to confront the fact that higher-status engineers, support workers, and supervisors view the workplace differently, can impose their definitions of work and learning upon others, and can discount the knowledge of production workers. The latter do not always accept the legitimacy of higher-status knowledge and repeatedly demonstrate its inadequacy, as well as the necessity for their own knowledge grounded in daily production work.

Workers thus live in a world of differentiated claims to knowledge in which they must necessarily recognize the claims of others. They acknowledge these claims by developing performances to be read by engineers and supervisors as evidence of commitment to superior knowledge, but they also develop "know-how" (Kusterer 1978) that allows them to meet production quotas. For their part, managers and engineers are not compelled to recognize multiple perspectives on work and learning because their own knowledge is privileged. The authority of Kramden's engineers is ultimately established by their jealously guarded control over the process, while management retains the power to arbitrarily hire and fire.

Workers, too, are situated precariously to press their claims of expertise. Not uncommonly they *are* incorrect about a point of fact due to the policy of control by ignorance, and their reputations suffer accordingly. Many adapt by remaining silent, and if they voice a valid claim they receive scant recognition. Instead, an engineering change order bearing the name of an engineer who had perhaps originally ridiculed their claim might suddenly appear, adding insult to injury from the perspective of the worker.

The fundamental point here is that in Kramden Computers, claims about knowledge, the relationship of knowledge to work, and the power to instruct are not merely pedagogical but are central to both work and workplace. Furthermore, knowledge is entangled with control on the production floor, which allows supervisors to ignore questions about motivations to instruct or learn: They simply command either to occur.

Our exploration of work and learning on the production floor has taken us far from the concept of skill requirements with its focus on the discrete abilities of individual workers or requirements of individual jobs. Understanding work and learning requires concepts quite different from those of task analysis and ability measurement, concepts that are emerging in research on social processes and individual action (Bernstein 1976; Bourdieu 1977; Engestrom 1987; Giddens 1979; Ortner 1984), learning and problem solving in natural settings (Lave 1988; Lave and Wenger 1991; Scribner 1984, 1986, 1992; Sternberg and Caruso 1985; Sternberg and Wagner 1986; Suchman 1987), and the social nature of cognition (Greeno 1988a, 1988b; Raizen 1989; Resnick, Levine, and Teasley 1991; Wertsch 1985). Here we relate our exploration of the production floor to the analytical tools needed to better understand the work and learning that occur there.

To begin, we found that some settings are formally defined as instructional, although learning is an inextricable part of all workplace practices. Instructional settings and a formal teacher's curriculum are neither irrelevant to learning in the workplace nor exhaustive of the possibilities for learning. However, formal curricula are not simply received but are interpreted by learners. These interpretations necessarily reflect work practices in ways that teachers may be unaware. Thus, work practices within specific workplaces may provide alternative lessons (Lave and Wenger 1991) that must be incorporated into an analysis of workplace learning. Understanding the relationships between divergent "curricula" is critical.

Learning on the production floor involves more than the internalization by learners of the knowledge presented by instructors (Lave and Wenger 1991). That knowledge is incompletely structured, and it may be of only limited utility to learners who confront problems unknown to the instructors. Contrary to Kramden's supervisors and engineers, working knowledge on the production floor is structured, but that structure emerges from the daily practices of assembling, testing, and repairing computers. Official pronouncements are incorporated into those practices, but workers do not simply internalize and then enact preexisting knowledge. Knowledge, too, is produced by the interactions among workers struggling to meet production quotas under conditions of incomplete information. All workplace denizens work as hard to establish claims to possess valid knowledge as they do to transmit that knowledge, although much working knowledge is tacit and unrecognized even by those who possessed it (Kusterer 1978). Explicating this tacit knowledge is a necessary part of any analysis of work.

Just as working knowledge is not simply the internalized representation of others' expertise, it is not static. Kramden's production workers interpret the demands made upon their learning by reference to a history of interactions with managers and engineers. Years of control by ignorance could not be overcome by the sudden pronouncement that workers were now vice presidents. Workers did not react with irrational skepticism; rather, they saw clearly that management itself had become so habituated to its power that the announced change would be impossible even if it were sincerely desired.

The importance of history lies not just in long-standing grudges, but in the gradual structuring of the workplace as well. Production technology builds upon previous efforts, as does a particular division of labor. Both can be other than they are. Manufacturing Sustaining engineers, for example, define their work as that of providing computerized information systems to reduce variances on the production floor, and not as developing documentation that is accessible to workers. This reflects the interests of their supervisor, a technological savant who works to automate production but who has scant interest in production work—or workers. Over the years he hired and trained three other engineers, and the department accordingly reflected his idiosyncratic understanding of its function.

Production work is more than merely the performance of tasks by isolated individuals, and learning involves much more than gaining the ability to perform required tasks. Work is conducted within a community of fellow practitioners, and becoming an effective worker means becoming part of that community. The community of practitioners has an internal organization built out of the division of labor on the production floor and the informal networks among workers, and it extends beyond the boundaries of the production floor into other departments and even companies where assemblers, test operators, and PCB technicians worked.

Production work in Kramden Computers also demonstrates that it is people who learn and produce computers, and not discrete bundles of skills. This might seem self-evident, but it is overlooked in the concept of skill requirements with its fragmentary view of the individual or job. However, the centering of the person in an analysis of work also implies a different model of thinking, one in which thinking is not coterminous with individual cognition. An increasing body of literature reflecting Vygotskian perspectives on cognition (Vygotsky 1978, 1986; Wertsch 1985) has established that contextual features are utilized in problem solving (Lave 1988; Scribner 1986) and that skilled performance is conditional on contextual sensitivity. Studies of mathematical competence (Balfanz 1990; Lave 1988; Saxe 1988;

Scribner 1986) indicate that people incorporate contextual features into their problem-solving activities, and often conceptualize and solve problems much differently than postulated by expert instructors. Reading at work is also undertaken with reference to specific features of the work setting (Diehl and Mikulecky 1980; Jacob 1986). Indeed, Brown, Collins, and Duguid (1989) argue that all cognition is situated and must be understood vis-à-vis a culture of learning.

How participation in work practices is structured in a specific workplace is thus critical for understanding work there. The experiences of Kramden's production workers suggest the need to explicate what people pay attention to, as well as those aspects of the workplace that are obscured, whether by accident or deliberate effort. Most important, practice in the workplace and workers' access to it is critical (Lave and Wenger 1991). We must avoid, however, thinking of workplace practice as a single idealized way to perform work, for the workplace may be differentiated along cleavages of power and interests. There is no reason to believe that there is in fact a single set of practices that provides a yardstick for assessing the mastery of workers. In this sense, practice is variable within the workplace and mastery is always partial.

The implications of this argument are far from comforting. If the concept of skill requirements poses dilemmas, so does the analysis of work practices. On the one hand, we may be comforted by empirical analyses replete with specific characteristics of technology and organization. These features may be described with great care, but any setting is subject to alternative descriptions so that other characteristics could be selected. Furthermore, empirical description of technology and work organization begs the question of how the specific characteristics chosen for analysis actually affect work and learning. Alternatively, we may attend to workers' accounts of work and their explanations of what they attend to. This may be revealing, but the ability of workers to account for their own performances is limited by the tacit nature of so much working knowledge and the operation of systems which affect work in ways unknown to them.

The concepts of a "community of practice" and "legitimate peripheral participation" reflect the relationship of work and learning we have been exploring. Lave and Wenger define a community of practice as "a set of relations among persons, activity, and world, over time and in relation with other tangential communities of practice" (Lave and Wenger 1991, 98). Legitimate peripheral participation acknowledges that newcomers master skill and knowledge by gradually increasing their participation in the socially organized practices of the community. Mastery is not simply a matter of task performance, nor is it based upon internalization of knowledge but rather upon becoming a full participant in a diverse community of copractitioners.

The concepts of community of practice and legitimate peripheral participation suggest an approach to understanding work and workplaces quite different from the concept of skill requirements. We may explore the roles of master and novice, or more broadly, the distribution of mastery within the community. The structure of access to participation and to mastery thus becomes critical. We may explore the social relationships among practitioners, and the cyclical development of the community as practitioners enter, move through it, and ultimately are replaced. Legitimate peripheral participation suggests that we analyze the differentiation of space, time, and knowledge within the workplace, and how people engage technology and formal procedures and policies. Learning how to talk within and about a community of practice becomes an important task for workers, and the process of increasing access to workplace practice can transform identities both as practitioners and people. Accordingly, the effects of participation on the self are explicitly addressed, as are questions of motivation to learn. Finally, we may attend to processes of change and contradiction within the community of practice, and not simply to the learning that occurs on the part of individual practitioners.

SUMMARY

Our journey across the production floor has brought us far from the tenets of skill requirements. Perhaps most notable is the far richer view of work that emerges from extended presence in the workplace, although describing work and workplace remain problematical. The utility of skills has been questioned, as well as the notion of unambiguous skill requirements of jobs or people. Thus, the workplace ethnography serves as a cautionary tale for those commentators who call for educational reforms that would make the school more like the workplace: we understand less about the latter than commonly assumed.

Our analysis of the production floor also suggests the outlines of an alternative analysis of work. Like any analysis, this one would necessarily be incomplete, but it addresses questions of how people learn to work. The workplace as a site of highly differentiated experiences and learning moves to center stage, with analysis of its specific characteristics and how they affect learning becoming paramount. Simultaneously, analysis shifts to the concept of work practice, its organization into a community of practice, and the process by which people increase their participation within that community.

Our journey through Kramden Computer's production floor is complete, and we now take the lessons learned and depart for the production floor of Calhoun Wire and Cable Company, a cavernous world of heavy machinery and loud noise. There we shift our focus from skills to workplace practices, and to the characteristics of the workplace itself. The world we encounter is far richer than one portrayed by the concept of skill requirements.

How do products move through the plant? Hmm, you know I don't know. That's hard to answer, because there's no one process that everything goes through. You might look in the lounge, though. There's a diagram, a model leaning against a wall there that they put together to show people how product was made. But there were so many things that didn't fit that the model was no use. Actually, I don't know that it's there anymore.

—Extruder operator

Calhoun Wire and Cable's production floor presents a striking contrast to that of Kramden Computers.[1] The latter is quiet except for the periodic "whoosh" of a computer being shoved down the rollers of an assembly line to its next destination, and the barely audible sound of music broadcast over a public address system. It presents itself as a clean, orderly array of assembly lines, punctuated by the ubiquitous terminals used to test and troubleshoot newly assembled computers and to record data about them as they are built. Calhoun's production floor, on the other hand, is gloomy and cavernous, a landscape of large machines and moving parts. Here, clanging bells, blaring pages to the telephone, and the din of machinery provide the punctuation.

Despite these and other differences, both workplaces have in common the appearance of chaos and unpredictability to newcomers, and of order and predictability to old-timers. Gradually, over months and years, the chaos fades and daily life becomes more predictable as the new arrival becomes familiar with the workplace. This predictability should not be mistaken for a complete understanding of the workplace, however, for while an old-timer's knowledge is extensive, it remains grounded in recurrent work experiences, the pronouncements of company officials, and the stories heard from colleagues elsewhere in the plant.

How newcomers gradually move from a state of initial confusion to one of comfort will be explored in Chapter 7. The present chapter describes how one new arrival, the anthropologist, confronted the buzzing confusion of the production floor. In the course of this discussion we will describe Calhoun Wire and Cable's landscape of machinery and products, and populate it with the operators who turn raw materials into specialized wires and cables. Our attention is directed to how the workplace reveals itself through its written documents, through the grand tours of departments and areas conducted by supervisors, and through operators' accounts of running machines. Specifically, we are concerned with how different methods of inquiry and sources of data shape the picture of work that emerges, and the implications of this picture for our understanding of work and learning.

CALHOUN WIRE AND CABLE COMPANY

Calhoun Wire and Cable is an operating division of Techno Industries, a corporation that develops technologies from basic research and then invents products using them to address customer problems. The corporation holds over 600 U.S. patents and has developed tens of thousands of products over its thirty-year history. It employed about 10,000 people when the fieldwork was conducted, and was divided into several groups of related research-manufacturing divisions. Calhoun Wire and Cable is the domestic manufacturing arm of one such division.

A stock purchase plan, credit union, profit sharing, medical plans, and life insurance are offered in a benefits package, and although wage data were not available to this study, the corporation has the reputation of paying wages typical for the industry. Techno Industries' educational assistance includes periodic on-site courses and an educational assistance program paying tuition and fees for employees who achieve a passing grade in courses leading to a degree in their field, improved work skills, or preparation for advancement.

The company views its corporate culture instrumentally: It is formally articulated and communicated through audiovisual aids and training presentations. Briefly, these emphasize risk taking in an "open environment." Bureaucracy and red tape are denigrated, and although conventional organizational charts exist they are not to be rigidly followed in decision making. Individuals with ideas, a stake in corporate outcomes, and a commitment to making things happen are expected to thrive in the culture, while those looking for rules, procedures, and clear career paths are warned that they may feel uncomfortable. The corporation claims to seek strong individuals who are able to work in groups, and the culture is oriented toward technical competence, creativity, willingness to stand up for one's convictions, commitment to the realization of new ideas and the success of the company, and finally, a willingness to communicate freely and openly. The relationship of this official version of corporate culture to life on the production floor will be touched upon in subsequent chapters.

Calhoun Wire and Cable is located near the corporate headquarters, and was one of its earliest operations. The company is housed in three contiguous buildings that were erected sequentially during the past thirty years, and it has the neat but worn appearance of a facility that has been overlooked as improvements were made elsewhere. Across the front of the buildings are offices housing administrative and support departments, such as Sales, Personnel, Manufacturing Engineering, and Production Control. Several conference rooms and a small lunchroom are also provided. Employees enter the plant through a small corridor with a rack of time cards; beyond are the doors that open onto the main aisle of a production floor that turns out wire and cable products around the clock, five or six days each week.

The production floor produces over five thousand products during a typical year, with specifications for thousands more available. While some of these products have been produced for years and their production is stable, other products are made infrequently, their chemical components change periodically, or they are made so seldom that sufficient learning to stabilize the process has not yet been achieved.

Like any workplace, this one has a specialized language that newcomers must master. Wire consists of a conductor surrounded by at least one layer of insulating material. Cables are comprised of at least two components, usually twisted around their longitudinal axes. Simple cables such as "twisted pairs" consist only of wires, while larger cables may be comprised of several smaller component cables, which in turn may have been built up from yet smaller ones. Large cables may contain hundreds of individual wires.

Cables may receive a protective sheath or "braid" over the components, and finally, an extruded layer of insulation (a "jacket"). Both wires and cables typically are identified by "marks" (letters, numbers, bands) made at intervals on the wire or cable surface. Alternatively, wires may be striped with one or more spirals of colored ink.

Orders of at least 100,000 feet of product are common, although only a few hundred feet of some specialized items are periodically produced. Calhoun Wire and Cable emphasizes producing a high-quality product that meets many exacting specifications. Representative physical specifications include the diameter of the wire or cable, the weight of a specified length, and its flexibility after exposure to environmental stresses such as heat or cold. The Quality Assurance Department exposes products to simple electrical tests to ensure that they can withstand power surges, and electrical continuity tests to detect faults in the components within a cable. Some products receive additional electrical tests, such as for impedance and capacitance.

Operators are encouraged to produce the longest possible lengths of products and to minimize production of "scrap" (defective wire). Should a product subsequently fail while being used, the extensive data collection performed by operators allows engineers to determine the precise conditions under which it was manufactured. This "traceability" is a source of competitive advantage, as is the company's reputation for meeting shipping deadlines. Products are shipped from the plant in specified "put-ups" and packaging. The former refers to the number of lengths of wire or cable placed on a spool, the size of the spool, how the ends of the product are to be handled, and so on. Packaging specifications are often detailed, idiosyncratic, and stringent.

The production floor, a nonunionized job shop, is populated by the "operations associates" (formerly called "machine operators," and now simply "operators") who are the focus of this and the next five chapters. Each operator is classified in one of four levels, depending on experience and competence, and assigned to one of four departments, each having a manager and supervisors for day, swing, and graveyard shifts. The departmental managers report to a production manager who, in turn, reports to Calhoun's plant manager. Most departments are subdivided into areas, and a few departments formally recognize highly experienced lead operators.[2]

Operators report directly to their shift supervisor, but they also interact with the other supervisors within their department since individual supervisors have responsibilities on all three shifts. For example, in the Extruding Department these duties are defined by product line and area: One supervisor is responsible for the Supreme Wire product line across all shifts, while another has similar responsibility for Large Cables. In another department the responsibilities are assigned exclusively by area: The day-shift supervisor is responsible for the Marking area on all shifts, the graveyard supervisor for Cabling, and the swing-shift supervisor for Shielding.

Working at Seeing

Calhoun Wire and Cable was in the midst of a projected five-year program of organizational change that had been initiated in response to increased competition in the specialized wire and cable market. The company had also just begun to upgrade its aging production technology. Because operators were widely viewed as possessing critical production-related knowledge, their participation in improving the production process was considered important by management, although the appropriate form of participation was hotly debated.

Techno Industries' Human Resources Department had been contacted about participating in the Educational Requirements for New Technology and Work Organization Project being conducted at Stanford University, and the department manager identified Calhoun Wire and Cable as a potential site for fieldwork. After several months of discussion about the scope of research, both Calhoun Wire and Cable and Techno Industries agreed to participate, and fieldwork began in early December 1987.

Relieved to find myself at a site that contrasted so sharply with Kramden Computers, I now faced the daunting prospect of learning about a workplace that welcomed my presence, but that did not cease operations while I oriented myself. After being introduced to the operators assigned to each department and being given a perfunctory half-hour tour of the plant, I was free to make my way among thundering machines of dubious functions.

This freedom was prized but it posed challenges for learning about a landscape that contrasted so markedly with Kramden Computers. In that site, products moved smoothly down the roller lines, the production process specifying what should occur along the way. Calhoun's production floor, on the other hand, was a job shop in which products took idiosyncratic paths through areas, often passing repeatedly through the same ones. Pattern was elusive here, and the very question of how a typical product passed through the plant was irrelevant, for there were no typical products. Months later I would witness lengthy meetings at which operators and supervisors from throughout the production floor attempted to trace the actual passage of a category of products through the plant in order to determine the consequences of introducing a new type of splice or machine. It was not the case, as in Kramden Computers, that no one really knew how products were manufactured—only that there was no single pathway that all products followed.

The anthropologist, or any outside observer, thus confronts the problem of making sense out of an unfamiliar world in the absence of a comprehensive description of it. We are necessarily forced to make observations about the production floor based on various sources of information. In the following sections we explore four alternative sources of information and their implications for understanding production work at Calhoun Wire and Cable. Gradually, our understanding enlarges, but it remains partial and distorted.

We begin our exploration with a stroll around the production floor. Two wide, parallel aisles connect the three contiguous buildings in which wire and cable is made, and between them are most of the machines used in that process. Smaller perpendicular aisles connect the main ones, dividing the floor into the areas of machines performing similar functions, such as adding an ink stripe or a protective braid.

Our stroll begins in the Materials area of Department 1000, where raw materials—conductor wire, pellets of insulating compound—are received by one or two operators and sent to the massive extruder machines which melt the compound and apply it as insulation to wires and cables. The extrusion process is the least stable in the plant, and the dozen or so operators per shift have traditionally comprised the aristocracy of the plant's operators. As we glance down the long aisles between these machines, we sometimes see several operators animatedly talking while they gesture to a machine, others intently completing paperwork, and some sitting idly with their eyes gazing off into the distance. Some machines appear abandoned, although wire continues to speed through the machine. A lone operator in the Tipping area removes defective sections of wire and cable, and splices the ends together in preparation for further processing.

Moving into the next building we find a dozen Department 2000 Packing operators sitting at their machines, patiently feeling every inch of wire or cable for defects. These operators cut out defects, and they complete much of the paperwork preparatory to shipping the order to customers. Unlike the extruder operators, who often seem to stray from their machines, these operators are seated at their work stations, fingers lightly gripping the wire as it passes alongside.

In the third building we find the three different areas of Department 3000. First we encounter a half dozen Marking area operators applying ink marks and stripes that identify products. Each operator is running two or three of the unique machines, which are topped by chimney-like ovens that bake the ink onto the wire or cable. Behind the Marking area are seven Cabling area operators who run the machines that twist components around their longitudinal axes, forming more complex cables. The machines are diverse, ranging from small machines that twist two wires together, to a large machine that twists up to thirty components around another cable.

As we wander back toward the starting point of our stroll, we encounter Department 3000's remaining area sandwiched between the extruders and spooling machines. This is the Shielding area, an area oddly out of place in the manufacture of specialized wire. Each of the seven operators is responsible for up to sixteen machines that were originally designed to make shoelaces, but adapted to weave a sheath of fine wire over cables. All are driven by pulleys from a common drive shaft; the clatter of metal parts is deafening and conversation is almost impossible. Across the aisle, two operators are working at the respool machines that supply the area with bobbins of the fine wire devoured each day by the other machines.

Throughout our stroll we notice several areas filled with ceiling-high racks stocked with reels of wire that are maintained by the Stocking Department. Its areas are dispersed throughout the plant and are generally staffed by one or two operators who transport reels of wire and cable to the other areas for further processing.

This then is the production floor. It is noisy and incomprehensible to the newcomer, who can barely understand the transformations performed in each area, much less the flow of materials between areas. It is a paradoxical world in which machine movement is ubiquitous—forklifts clanging, cabling machine wheels turning, shielding machines hypnotically revolving—but where humans seem strangely inert. Precisely what the work of running a machine *is* remains obscure, as does the organization of the production floor.

Grand Tours

Hoping to find out more about the work of making wire and cable, we next undertake "grand tours" in which supervisors describe the important features of their departments or of specific areas within them. Homer, the day-shift supervisor responsible for Department 1000, conducts such a tour of the Extruding area.

I meet Homer in the Department 1000 supervisor's office. He explains that orders are scheduled by the Extruding scheduler after Production Control sends him the packet of documents needed to initiate and complete processing of a product. The packet consists of a production order that defines the route the product will take through the production floor, a materials list that specifies the amounts of materials to be used in processing it, and a manufacturing specification document that describes in detail the operations to be performed at each machine.

The scheduler then prepares three other documents used by the operators. Homer reminds me that this system of documentation is used for only one product line; he has worked to condense the plethora of paperwork into a single "cost center report" initiated by the scheduler and completed by the operators as they process each order. He laughs and asks if I am confused yet. I concur, and he says, "Don't worry, it'll get clearer." The scheduler shakes his head and winks.

We leave the office and head for the Materials area. Homer pauses in the large entrance door and says, "This is where it all comes from," and then quickly leads me through the area, pointing out the storage racks of pelleted insulating compound and conductor wire, the scales used to weigh the compound, and ovens used to dry it before it is sent to the extruders. We stroll by a desk, where he points to baskets for paperwork and the presence of a computer terminal. This portion of the tour takes less than five minutes.

We exit by a second door and walk directly to Extruder #1. A bundle of paperwork rests on the nearby workbench and Homer separates it into five separate piles. "This is what the operator works off of," he remarks. A single machine load list itemizes the orders assigned to the machine each shift, but the operator will arrange them in a "commonsense sequence, depending on the time each takes, its priority, and the color." The paperwork has been partially completed in red ink by the scheduler, and the operator will complete each form in black ink as the orders are completed. The page has dozens of boxes in which the operator records data about the materials he used, the product, and the conditions under which it was run.

Homer explains the numerical system for coding reels ("It's simple, and once you know it you know exactly what's on the reel, the date it was processed, and even whether it was the first or second or third reel and so on that was processed on that machine that day"), but I have trouble following the explanation. He laughs and says, "It is a little much, but remember that it used to be worse before I condensed a lot of this stuff."

He gestures to the extruder and identifies a few parts but quickly returns to the bundle of paperwork. "Here the operator takes samples of the wire every 5,000 or 10,000 feet—it's specified—and enters the fault codes for each increment. Then he enters the lot number of the compound used and the temperature of the head, the face plate, collar, hopper. All the different zones. All the readings are taken from [pointing] that panel. Oh, and he measures the wall, too." I ask about the latter measurement and he explains that the wall refers to the thickness of the insulation on the conductor, which is specified in the paperwork. "You'll figure it out soon. It just takes some time." Homer turns and says, "C'mon."

We walk over to a collection of reels containing cables that Homer identifies as the Shielding queue. These cables await the application of an insulating jacket of compound before being shipped to customers or being incorporated into larger cables. "The Shielders roll these reels over here when they're done with them and tag each reel [points to a pink tag on a reel] to indicate it's new to the queue. One of our operators takes the paperwork off the reel and stamps the material list [points to an imprint on a material list]. He leaves the paper in that basket at the front of the queue, and then it's pulled and jacketed. Then it gets sent to Tipping for splicing."

Homer describes the paperwork for two other product lines as we stroll to the Tipping area. He points to a basket labeled "Tipping In," where operators receive their orders, and a queue containing six filled reels. "When they're done they put a Tipping Feedback Card on the reel and leave the paperwork in one of those [points to four] boxes that are used to schedule the next step." Homer explains that the "customer operator," who next receives the reel, fills in the Tipping Feedback Card and returns it to the Extruding lead operator who routes it to the Tipping operator. The card is used to record information about the quality of the splices made by the Tipping operator.

As we leave Tipping, Homer points to an area against the wall that is the Extruding lead desk, where operators receive their daily assignments, although most operators are assigned the same machine for about six months at a time. We complete our hour-and-fifteen-minute stroll by passing through other machines, where Homer presents a similar description of paperwork and machinery, albeit with less detail. With a laugh, he asks if I have any questions and concludes with "It'll get clearer in a while."

Within a week I received grand tours of other departments and areas, each of which followed a similar pattern. The resulting descriptions were built around several elements. First, typical pieces of machinery were described in global terms, such as "That's a shielder. It puts a braid in the cable." Some tour guides also described basic machine parts such as the "payoff," "dancer," and "sparker." Second, a flow of materials to and from the department or area was traced, although there were usually gaps in the routes traced. Third, a typical packet of paperwork that accompanied each order and that the operator "worked off of" was reviewed, always accompanied by apologies like "This probably doesn't make much sense to you yet." Finally, a flow of paperwork paralleling the flow of material was described. Generally, the bundles of paperwork and their movement through the area were described in more detail than the actual processing that machines performed in the area.

These descriptions seem obvious and natural, precisely what we would expect of a manufacturing supervisor. Yet it is their very naturalness to which we must pay attention, for our tour guides told stories that represented the workplace in a particular way. Each guide utilized a set of physical landmarks—machinery and documents—to tell a story, thereby directing our attention toward technology and away from people and work organization. In effect, a subtle technological bias was built into the very act of touring an area.

Work organization was largely invisible and could not be seen in the same direct manner as were machinery and paperwork. While formal work organization was easily captured in formal organizational charts, evidence of the informal organization of work was scattered in months of field notes and was only gradually inferred with considerable effort. It was invisible to supervisors and operators, too, although the former freely admitted that the production floor was, as one remarked, "different from this [holding up an organizational chart of his department]; a completely different world out there."

The tour accounts also described paperwork and material flowing largely as they should. The whirlpools, eddies, and rapids that characterized Kramden Computer's much simpler production process were seemingly absent here: Orders simply flowed between areas and through machines and then to customers without pause.

Finally, most tours reflected the interests of the particular guide. Homer had recently condensed a half dozen documents into one; thus, the inordinate attention he devoted to paperwork. Jill, another supervisor, was concerned with safety issues and conducted a tour that focused on that topic.

Again, these accounts undoubtedly make sense to us: We must understand "the basics" before we can understand the complexities of the workplace. However, the important methodological point must not be lost: If we content ourselves with the basics, managing the complexities of work remains opaque to us. And managing that complexity is at the heart of the operator's job. As we will see in later chapters, prolonged study of Calhoun Wire and Cable revealed more detail about the work of operators, but it also opened up entirely new dimensions of the workplace: The tour accounts were not only selective and partial, but distorted as well.

Operator Accounts of Work

Next, we turn to the operators themselves for insight into their work. Representative descriptions of work in the Extruding and Marking areas are presented in order to paint a more detailed picture of production work, as well as to indicate how operators typically describe their jobs.

We begin by summarizing a discussion with Wayne, a veteran operator, who is running an order of wire on Extruder 40. The extruder is actually comprised of several discrete components arrayed along sixty feet of the production floor. Extruder 40 faces another extruding machine allowing Wayne and its operator, Rafael, to share a workbench between them. When I comment on the size and complexity of the machine, Wayne responds, "It's big, but basically it's pretty simple," and he walks over to one end where a motorized axle holds a four-foot-diameter reel of conductor wire. Several feet forward is an elaborate contraption of pulleys supported by a metal post bolted to the concrete floor. Pointing to the axle Wayne explains, "This is the pay-off where we load the conductor wire. Then it gets strung up through the dancer." He traces a pattern around the pulleys with his hand. A few feet ahead the wire, which is whizzing by at hundreds of feet per minute, enters a die and emerges with a layer of molten plastic being drawn down to cover it. It immediately enters a fifteen-foot-long trough of water, passes through several metal boxes, and then wraps around two large wheels which are pulling the wire off the pay-off reel.

As I stare at the cone of compound formed as the wire emerges from the die, Wayne comments, "That's the head and there's the tooling. You install that, a die and nipple, specially for your order. And screen pack, too." When I ask which is the head, Wayne explains, "The head is that big part on the end of the faceplate that goes across the end of the screw and barrel. The tooling is held in place by the collar that bolts in place in the head. After I set up the tooling for an order, you string the conductor wire through the dancer and then thread it through the head. That's the barrel and the screw is inside turning and melting and forcing the compound out through the tooling." Without looking away from me, Wayne reaches into the water trough and lightly rolls the moving wire between his fingers. Suddenly, he points to a hopper on top of the barrel, walks to the rear of the extruder and climbs a ladder in order to peer into it. Returning a moment later, he comments, "You can't run out of compound when you're in an order."

Back of the trough is a massive console, about eight feet high and fifteen feet long. It is covered with an intimidating array of meters, gauges, knobs, and dials that Wayne scarcely looks at. I ask him about their functions, and he says most of them control the heaters that warm different sections of the barrel in order to melt the compound pellets. Pointing at several gauges he says, "That's what you really watch. The line speed, how fast the wire is moving. And the barrel pressure and the screw RPMs [rotations per minute]. I mainly look at the cone [points to the compound emerging from the tooling], and how the wire feels. If it's rough." Rafael, who has been observing this encounter with obvious amusement, asks if I want to know how he monitors the product, and then points to the clock on the wall and laughs: "That's the only gauge I look at."

Wayne concludes the tour by explaining the functions of the mysterious metal boxes. The sparker detects defects in the insulation and the electronic micrometer measures the diameter of the wire as it speeds by. The extruder terminates at a second dancer around which the wire is strung and finally a "take-up" reel receives the completed product.

Wayne reiterates that the machine is "basically simple," and that running it consists of "loading the pay-off," "setting the tensions" on the dancer, "setting up the tooling," "setting the run conditions" (temperatures, speeds, screw rotations), "stringing up wire through the dancers," "threading it through the head," and "adjusting the machine" while it runs. He shakes hands and says, "Come on back anytime if you have any questions." I try to shake life into a hand cramped from writing, and head off to another area.

Operator accounts of work in other areas followed a similar pattern. Samuel, a Marking area operator, stood by a machine and talked while nervously eyeing the two others he was operating that day. "You get your paperwork [waving a plastic envelope crammed with documents] and the tooling you need comes with it. Then you find the reel over there in that queue and roll it to the pay-off. Load it and set up the tooling, add the ink to the pan and make sure it's mixed. Set your heats [i.e., the ovens attached to each machine]." Pointing to the machine that is running, he says, "Once you're ready to go you string it up through the dancer, through the marking wheel and up the oven, and then down through a dancer and the pay-off. Pretty simple, but you have to spend some time getting the wheel and wipe adjusted just right. And you have to keep watching them in case the wire gets knocked off the wheel by a splice. Ramp up the machine to the speed you want and that's it."

Descriptions of machines and machine operation are similar, at least partially because the machines are built from similar components.[3] Reels of wire or cable are positioned on one of several types of pay-offs, devices that raise the reel, allowing product to pay off it. Tasks here are loading and unloading the pay-off reel.

Immediately in front of the pay-off is a dancer, a series of adjustable pulleys around which the wire is wound. A variety of dancers is utilized, differing mainly in the means of controlling the tension placed on the wire, but all function to reduce variations in tension (i.e., tautness) of the wire. The tasks associated with the dancer are stringing up the product around the dancer's pulleys and setting the pressure on its arms.

Next, the product passes through a tooling head that performs the operation, for example, an extruder die and nipple or a marking machine wheel and ink well. These operations define the different areas of the plant, although they generally require setting up (installing the correct gears, dies, nipples, guides, marking wheels, and other parts), loading the machine with product and inputs to the process (e.g., compound, inks, tapes), running the order, making adjustments, and cleaning up afterward.

The transformed product usually passes through one of several sparkers that detect faults or breaks in the insulation. The product then runs to a revolving take-up device that pulls the product off the pay-off. Alternatively, capstans positioned between the operating head and take-up device pull the product through the process. The work of stringing up continues until the operator has positioned the product around the take-up reel.

To the newcomer, including the anthropologist, the number of machine controls is daunting, although operators mentioned little about them except that their basic tasks were to monitor and adjust their machines. Both monitoring and adjusting were presented as simple tasks in which conditions of the machine (e.g., temperatures, speeds, and tensions), and states of the product (e.g., rough insulation, illegible mark) are detected and compensating adjustments are made by changing machine settings: pulling and releasing clutch levers, turning dials (e.g., potentiometers or "pots"), pressing buttons, positioning dies and nipples, and changing gears.

Operator accounts of work such as Wayne's and Samuel's are thus patterned. They present work as "basically simple," with many operators adding that there is "not much to say about it." The work is decomposed into a set of clear, discrete, and step-like tasks, such as verifying (paperwork), stringing up (the wire or cable), and monitoring (the order being processed). Those operators who did mention interruptions to the smooth processing of orders spoke of troubleshooting as a rational, step-by-step procedure that inevitably terminated in finding the fault's cause and a good solution. Intuition and failures were never mentioned.

Asking operators to describe their work on the production floor clearly enriches our understanding of work, but the typical pattern of such accounts piques our curiosity about their work. What is omitted from their accounts is at least as revealing as what is included. Paperwork and documentation are seldom mentioned in these accounts; direct engagement with the machine is the "work." Yet we notice that the production floor is awash in paperwork and continuous efforts are made to manage it.

Processing generally proceeds as intended, and diagnosing problems and taking corrective actions are not discussed. However, operators are constantly discussing problems with specific products and ways to troubleshoot recalcitrant machines or products. Activities that are physically removed from the machines, such as attending meetings, are never recounted, although supervisors describe ubiquitous department, area, and special project team meetings.

Finally, operators describe their work as proceeding largely in isolation from other operators: The engagement of operator and machine is paramount. Yet when a problem does arise, a cluster of operators soon converges on the site, some to offer advice and others to ascertain information. Help comes in less dramatic ways, too. Wayne, the veteran extruder operator, later said that he had hurried to add compound pellets to the hopper because a distant operator had alerted him by clutching his throat, the signal that a hopper is almost empty.

Thus, operator accounts of work are essential sources of information about work, and their very form hints at a larger world of work that they rarely articulate. Our picture of work and the workplace is now more detailed and refined, but it remains selective in important ways that we barely understand.

Documentation and Work

Our final source of information about the production floor is provided by procedures that describe how work is to be performed and other documentation that describes the characteristics of the people who perform it. We begin with the binders of procedures found in each department, many of which contain dozens of pages describing sequences of tasks.

Some procedures describe how to process one product in the area (e.g., "Marking a Supreme 100 Cable"), while many describe facets of operating an area's machines, such as installing tooling, loading a heavy reel onto a pay-off device, or stringing up the product. For example, an Extruding procedure describes several sequential tasks in cleaning the barrel of the machine. To remove part of the tooling, the operator should

> Pry out core tube using wooden block and wrench. Secure bottom of tube in vise. Brush off with steel brush, then wipe off with rag. Remove nipple using 6" crescent wrench, turning counterclockwise. Replace nipple using same procedure.

Such procedures may be comprised of twenty or thirty discrete steps, some spelled out in painstaking detail, others more general (e.g., "Reassemble tooling"). Other procedures prescribe operator movements in detail, such as the following excerpt from a procedure for cutting fast moving wire: "Grasp wire with grasping hand, cut wire with cutting hand in back of grasping hand. With rotation of reel, wrap wire with grasping hand back on reel. With cutting hand, traverse wire back over flaying end."

Procedures commonly take the form of checklists to be used with each order. The Marking area checklist, for example, consists of fourteen measurements or inspections that the operator makes in the course of processing each order. Most checklists are similar since they require the operator to compare properties of the raw materials and finished product with written specifications. Other checklists require the operator to enter data describing the machine settings used to process the order; the Extruding paperwork developed by Homer constitutes such a checklist. By their very format checklists order the measurements or inspections made by the operator, but this ordering is limited. Checklists rarely specify the sequence in which data should be entered, although some ask the operator to enter data before, during, and after processing the order.

Other procedures address episodic events such as "Aligning the Marker Head," or they provide guidance for the operator confronted with problems in processing an order (e.g., "Troubleshooting Tips"). This is especially elaborated in Extruding. For one product line, eight problems, such as "surface roughness," "wall too light," or "die drool," are identified, each followed by two to five possible remedies. The latter are brief admonitions such as "decrease RPM," "check water temperature," and "wrong set-up." Other "procedures" are actually reference tables for converting units of measurement, estimating the capacity of an empty reel, or selecting tooling such as gears or pulleys to achieve a specified result.

Procedures are thus heterogeneous, although several common features are noteworthy. First, they are often presented as step-like sequences of actions that, if followed closely, produce a specific outcome. For example, when using the especially combustible materials to extrude GEECO, an infrequently produced cable, Leo places a two-page procedure on his workbench. With seventeen clearly defined steps, he calls it "my recipe," and as he completes each step he lightly pencils a check mark next to it. When the order is complete, he erases the check marks and returns the procedure to its place in a binder.

Most other procedures bear a looser connection to the action they describe. The concluding comment in a Cabling area procedure captures this sentiment:

> In general, all operating manuals are a starting point, or an outline for a known procedure. Each operator will probably do some things a little different.

The operator is thus expected to follow the known procedures, but according to operators and supervisors, the operator is ultimately responsible for the output from his machine. If an unsatisfactory product results, he is expected to modify the run conditions or stop the machine until expert advice is obtained. Eric, a Marking operator, noted:

You can't hide behind a procedure or that someone, even a supervisor, told you to do something if it doesn't make sense. You can't hide behind the paperwork if it doesn't make sense. Like putting a really small mark on a humongous cable. Everyone knows you don't do that. You gotta show common sense.

Second, the step-like procedures presume considerable background knowledge by the operator, as well as the discrete, separable nature of each step. The admonition to "center the die," for example, glosses over a series of adjustments the Extruding operator makes that constitute this task. Brief observations of operators reveal that each instance of centering requires slightly different torques and sequences of adjustments to several bolts until, as operators report, the die "looks right." Even after starting the extruder, the operator may perform further adjustments and centering the die may occur throughout the run.

Troubleshooting recommendations, in particular, presume considerable operator knowledge. In utilizing the Extruding troubleshooting guide cited above, the operator must initially determine that the product is less than satisfactory (either failing to meet specifications or the operator's own personal standard of "good product"), interpret its characteristics as evidence of a specific problem, and select from the suggested solutions one that is likely to rectify the problem. How these choices are to be made is not specified, and the operator is cautioned, "Whenever you use any of the above recommendations to correct a problem, remember that each one will always affect your overall dimension." The importance of an operator's background knowledge is also revealed in the checklists and reference tables, neither of which provide step-like models for action, although each item may well be sequentially numbered.

Conversations with veteran operators revealed that they rarely referred to procedures while running an order. However, an operator may appear to be following the written procedure when in fact she is only performing actions that correspond to those that are written, often because the operators have written the procedure in the first place. Although we can conclude the operator is acting consistently with known procedures, it is erroneous to assert that she is *following* the written procedure; in fact, she may be unaware of its existence.

If procedures are so seldom used, we may fairly ask why they are constantly being developed and revised. Procedures are utilized primarily in training new operators, a topic to which we will return in Chapter 7, although there are other motivations for developing procedures. In several cases, products or machines were so inconsistently operated as to alarm engineers or supervisors who sought to standardize operation by developing a procedure. Many supervisors, too, are recent college graduates who are initially overwhelmed by the complexity of their departments, and who wish to increase their knowledge of and control over the production floor by developing procedures.

A final motivation is that of presenting the workplace as a rationally organized facility, one in which it is possible to demonstrate the company's control over the production process. Homer, the Extruding supervisor, had lobbied hard for procedures that would ultimately provide a basis for certifying operators to handle specific products or operate specific machines. He explained, "If a customer is on a tour and asks, 'How do I know you can produce this or that?' I want to be able to take a procedure down off the machine and show him that that operator knows it. Right there."

In summary, the binders of procedures are inconsistent and heterogeneous, and fail to provide a complete and exhaustive picture of work in an area. Instead, work is presented as a series of discrete, unambiguous steps that are rationally organized to bring about a predictable outcome. Alternatively, many documents nominally categorized as procedures fail to provide any sequential ordering.

The lesson here is not that the production floor is chaotic, with each operator proceeding as he or she wishes, but rather that known procedures are simply not recorded on paper or transmitted by reading, and thus what is written bears a complex and indirect relationship to the operators' work. Comments such as Eric's about the need for common sense, and the widespread remarks, both written and oral, that procedures are merely guidelines or starting points suggest that the reality of work on the production floor is far more complex than suggested by the terse instructions of the procedures (Orr 1991).

If procedures prescribe work, skill matrices, employee manuals, and performance review forms prescribe workers. The Product 6000 Team Member Checklist is such a document, one intended to prescribe and assess team members along fourteen variables such as technical competence, planning and organizing, responsibility, comfort with machinery, hard work, team player, flexible, and interest in the job. Team members are rated satisfactory or unsatisfactory on each variable, and examples of each are provided. For example, an unsatisfactory rating on responsibility is exemplified by being "defensive," "blames others," and "resentful," while "automatically accepts responsibility" exemplifies satisfactory performance.

Such skill matrices provide useful insights into their authors' models of successful workers, but they leave much unanswered. The exemplars of satisfactory and unsatisfactory performance require clarification. For example, the extremes of "interest" in the job are exemplified by "passing time" versus "wants to work here." These presumably correlate with a set of behaviors through which the operator can be assessed. However, we must clarify why these particular fourteen variables were selected, what counts as satisfactory or unsatisfactory performance on each, how operators learn to orchestrate performances directed at achieving better ratings, and their incentives to do so. The status of such documents is also often unclear. Although the matrix is couched in descriptive terms, it is implicitly normative: Operators *should* "want to work here," be "respectful and helpful," and "have a sense of humor." As normative models of the production floor, such documents cannot be ignored, but in order to understand how work is performed we must be grounded in description: What skills *are* manifested in the performance of work?

Documents such as these may in some cases describe actions, but they are also used to justify actions. For example, when one operator was accused of "covering up" a misdeed committed by an operator on another shift, he pleaded that he was only trying to be "supportive of team members." Thus, he drew upon a formally recognized exemplar of the "satisfactory team player" in order to account for his actions. Several operators, too, commented that skill matrices could be used to punish unpopular workers during performance reviews. Arthur, for example, angrily displayed his latest performance review that rated his participation as unsatisfactory because he seldom contributed in meetings, refused to train new workers, and was difficult to get along with. "What do they mean, 'Not participating'! I've been here over twenty years: *That's* participation. I come in whenever they want." For Arthur, and for other operators, the issue is not simply the fairness of a rating, but rather which behaviors even constitute a basis for assessment.

Like the written procedures, skill matrices and similar documents provide a partial description of the worker. Subsequent fieldwork indicated that they are frequently drawn upon by supervisors and operators alike to press claims that someone is or is not working effectively. They also occasionally serve to focus discussions in departmental meetings, as when a supervisor asked, "What does it mean to be a 'team player' in our department?," provoking a thirty-minute discussion among the operators. Supervisors concur that much of importance is left out of such matrices, and they are subject to numerous challenges in interpretation. Despite disagreements about their content and application, such documents do provide a standard to which operators, with varying degrees of consensus, should aspire. But they do not describe how workers are skilled, only how they should be skilled from one point of view.

SEEING THE WORKPLACE

We have explored four ways of seeing the workplace. Each constitutes a reasonable way to begin learning about Calhoun Wire and Cable, but each is limited in the perspective it provides. Here we review the characteristic picture of work that emerges from our initial excursions in learning. Subsequent fieldwork modified this picture by providing more details about tasks, machines, and roles, but also by opening entirely new vistas for scrutiny.

First, our sketch of the workplace is based upon a very limited sample of observations, resulting in a distorted view of the production floor. Because of our unfamiliarity with the workplace and the desire of supervisors and operators to communicate the basics, single ways to perform nominally identical tasks are identified. We thereby fail to explore the possibility of diverse strategies for performing tasks and so analysis converges on a single set of skills.

The grand tours, worker accounts of their jobs, and documentation all suggest a workplace where things work largely as they should, thereby directing our attention away from interruptions to the smoothly operating workplace. Strategies to manage variances are seen as peripheral to the basics if they are recognized at all. Rare or unique events that must be managed by operators go unreported, and instead we see routine, ordinary events, although according to supervisors the hallmark of the skilled operator is the ability to handle infrequent occurrences.

A related bias is especially critical: By focusing on production-related tasks, we fail to see events that take days, weeks, or perhaps even months or years to unfold. In particular, operator involvement in long-term projects is lost with the focus on "getting the product out the door" (i.e., production-related tasks). The potentially different set of skills involved in such projects, especially those designed to improve the workplace, remains undetected. This is a significant omission, since the latter skills may be communicative, social, or organizational in nature.

There is also a likely tendency to underestimate the difficulty in mastering some tasks, not only because of the focus on the basics, but also because the workplace tends over time to be populated by those people who are successful at mastering the tasks. The actual effects of this bias are unclear, but it is important to note that our informants are precisely those people who have survived in the workplace, and their bias may be toward discounting their own abilities.

The workplace also appears as a rational instrument carefully designed to accomplish specific ends. What matters about such a workplace can be described in terms of the disembodied process we encountered at Kramden Computers: Human agency appears irrelevant to the real work of the production floor. It is the process that seems to create technical exigencies, which in turn drive tasks and skills. Operators simultaneously follow known procedures in order to be categorized as efficient, but they are compelled to deviate from them if common sense suggests they do so. How operators balance these conflicting demands remains unclear, as does the relationship between the normative and descriptive nature of procedures.

Another quality of our picture of work is that it is quite crisp, clear, and certain, but not fully detailed. What occurs on the production floor is described by a set of tasks and roles that are well-specified and unambiguous. These tasks and roles must be executed in order to complete the operations of making wire and cable. Because these tasks and roles are so clearly specified, we may believe that operators can be trained to perform them. In fact, training and the operation of the workplace come together in on-the-job training or learning, in which operator experiences are derived directly from the exigencies of task and role performance. The workplace effectively teaches lessons that, if operators can only learn, results in an efficient operation. From this perspective, formal training programs and informal on-the-job learning provide valid and reliable lessons, and they account for how operators learn how to perform their jobs.

Finally, the workplace is described in seemingly natural, universal categories so that the resulting descriptions may be generalized across sites. Terms such as *training, skill,* or *mechanical ability* are freely used, and they provide a set of context-free concepts we can use to organize our thinking about the workplace.

There are, however, pitfalls in accepting such concepts at face value, as illustrated by the skill of mechanical ability. The first weeks on the production floor revealed that many operators and supervisors believe this ability to be critical. Yet subsequent discussions revealed several discrepant definitions of mechanical ability. For some operators, it is the ability to understand the workings of a machine and to diagnose causes of failure. For others, the emphasis is on problem solving, regardless of whether a machine is involved. Several other operators defined it as the ability to "feel comfortable" around moving machinery and to be "hands on" learners.

Likewise, concepts like training and teams are subject to local definition. Many operators, for example, reported they were trained, but further conversations revealed that some meant "I am adequately trained in all aspects of operating this machine," while the comments of others suggested a different meaning: "I have received whatever constitutes training in this area." Alternatively, to have been a trainer constituted very different things in different areas.

In effect, the problem of meaning we identified with the skills matrices was writ large on the workplace. Although a common language was spoken, important concepts differed in meaning throughout the plant. This suggests limits on generalizing terms across sites without accompanying exploration of what each term denotes in each site, and it demonstrates the importance of local processes in the workplace that define the content of seemingly neutral, objective concepts.

Our initial excursion thus has the effect of leaving us feeling more confident in our understanding of the production floor, although further details would be useful. Ironically, this certitude fades the more we explore daily life on the production floor and find a world of work far richer than suggested by our initial sketch. In order to understand this world we must distinguish between description and analysis of how operators work, and the often veiled claims about how they should or must be working. We must understand how operators actually learn to produce complex wires and cables on actual machinery, and not content ourselves with the explanation that they were trained to do so. And we must understand how the operators participate in the community of practice in their workplace. In order to do so, we must leave the comfortable realm of quick excursions and tidy accounts of work, and observe the actual practices of machine operators.

5 NUTS AND BOLTS

It's really pretty simple here. You just look at the paperwork, load the machine, and make sure your set-up is right. Then run it.
—Marking operator

It takes years to become really good here. You can get a machine up and running real soon. But you have to be able to handle everything and lots of things we don't run except every few years.
—Another Marking operator

In this chapter we deepen our exploration of the production floor by meeting some of the operators and talking with them at length while they run their machines. In Chapter 4 we saw that brief interviews with operators, grand tours of areas, and reviews of written documentation provided valuable information, but they also resulted in very selective images of production work that raise as many questions as they answer. In this chapter we flesh out our picture by presenting case studies of work practices in two areas, Extruding and Cabling. Extruding is the most unstable process performed in the plant, and its operators have traditionally been at the apex of the production-floor social hierarchy. Although engineers and operators alike claim that the principles underlying the process are simple, the conversion of pelleted insulation into its molten form is concealed from the operator's view, thereby presenting the basic conceptual challenge of the job. Cabling provides a vivid contrast, since the process is very stable and visible to the operator. Later, we will see this visible process transformed when a state-of-the-art, computerized cabling machine was commissioned.

Our case studies focus on the characteristics of machines and materials, and the strategies operators use to "make product." The discussion is necessarily detailed in order to capture the specific characteristics of machines and materials that affect the operator's job. But we also explore how the practices of operators are structured by their attempts to manage ubiquitous variances in materials and machines, and by the functioning of a larger system of feedback between areas.

Two themes are evident in our discussion. First, the operator does not engage a world in general, but rather the very specific characteristics of machines and materials that pose threats to production, and thus, to his or her job. Developing a sensitivity to the contextual features of the work environment and finding ways to manage variance in machines and materials is essential to the operator. In Chapter 7, we explore how a larger system of feedback relationships among areas shapes practices as much as do the specific characteristics of machines.

Second, there are no purely instrumental challenges to the operator, for production work is deeply embedded in a nexus of social relationships and cultural meanings. Thus, the operator does much more than master technical skills: He or she enters a community of practice.

Case Study: Extruding

We may explore the practice of extruding by following an operator as he runs several orders during his shift. John has been "into" an order on Extruder 33 for nearly an hour when I arrive. John has been an extruding operator for six years and has an excellent reputation among the supervisors and other operators who speak of his discipline and organization. John is inspecting the paperwork for his next order when suddenly he taps his head and says, "An alarm just went off." He turns and walks briskly to the control panel, where he glances at the footage counter: He says he is within 2,000 feet of the end of the order. He rotates the "pot" that controls the capstans pulling the wire from the pay-off reel in order to slow ("ramp down") the extruder until it stops.

He reaches into his pocket and takes out a wire cutter, which he uses to cut the wire near the extruder head. The wire lies limp in the trough of water that cools the newly insulated wire as it leaves the tooling. He pulls the bare conductor back through the head and clips off several feet, tossing it into a "scrap bucket." He winds the remaining unused conductor back on the pay-off reel, ejects it from the pay-off axle, and rolls it aside. When the next order is "up 'n running," he will roll it to the Stocking area so it can be restocked.

John loads a new reel of conductor wire on the pay-off and then inspects it. The paperwork that accompanies the order specifies the diameter of the conductor wire, as well as the number and diameter of each strand comprising the wire. The copper conductor is coated with one of several metals such as tin or nickel, which impart particular properties to the wire. For example, while tin copper conductor is smooth and easy to handle, nickel copper conductor is stiff and winds back on itself, making it difficult for the operator to handle. Some conductors, too, are rough and result in a bumpier insulation despite the operator's best efforts. Conductor wire is supplied by several manufacturers, each of which have reputations among the extruder operators for producing wire of certain quality. John verifies that the conductor is that specified and says it should be easy to run as he strings it up through the wheels of the pay-off dancer. Meanwhile, molten compound oozes through the tooling and drops into a bucket. John pokes the conductor through the nipple and then seizes the free end with pliers on the other side. He pulls it through, ties it to the end of the wire resting in the trough, and then returns to the control panel where he gradually ramps up the extruder.

John glances every few seconds at the laser micrometer that continuously measures the diameter of the newly insulated wire. He slowly turns up the "speed pot" so that the wire passes faster through the tooling, thereby reducing the thickness of the insulation. In addition to the speed pot, John says he can vary the rotations per minute of the extruder screw that forces the compound through the tooling, and the temperatures of the heaters attached to nine areas of the extruder barrel and tooling. "Usually, you just set the heat profile and leave it alone. You know it from memory, or some guys use the fact sheets that are on file. Or you can ask someone who's run the product recently."

Once he judges that the product is running well, John walks to the pair of take-up reels at the end of the machine where the wire is being wrapped onto the reel holding the previous order. John loads an empty reel on the second take-up device and bangs the large push button to start the new take-up reel. He pulls the wire cutters from his pocket, quickly grabs the wire that is speeding past, cuts it, and in one motion, wraps it around the empty reel. He completes the tasks by slapping the stop button on the first take-up reel. The entire operation has taken several seconds. "'Cutting on the fly' is intimidating at first," he says, "but it's automatic after a while, although some guys still feel uncomfortable doing it at really high speeds."

With the finished reel stopped, he cuts a sample of wire and trots to a workbench equipped with several test instruments. He weighs the length of wire and then places it in a device that stretches the wire to measure its elasticity. Then he cuts a thin cross-section of insulation and places it under a microscope, where he checks that the conductor is centered in it. As he works, he enters the measurements on the paperwork attached to the order.

The data entered, he returns to the take-up reel holding the completed order and manually unwraps the several thousand feet of wire he had added to it before switching the present order to its new reel. When he reaches the knot he had tied, he cuts the wire, discards the scrap wire, performs the measurements on the completed order, and "closes the paperwork." Finally, he rolls the completed reel with the attached documentation to the Tipping area.

John completes two other orders in similar fashion when, after scrutinizing the next order, he announces, "I gotta change my set-up." In addition to new tooling, the insulation on the new order is cream-colored, necessitating a "cleanout" to remove the darker color he has been using. Cleanouts are also performed at regular intervals to remove contaminants from the extruder barrel. I ask if he chooses when to clean out the machine, and he replies that cleanouts are scheduled, but "an efficient operator can juggle orders to do it when it makes sense."

When the current order is complete, John stops the capstan and the wire droops into the water trough. The revolving screw continues to push compound through the barrel and he climbs up to the hopper in order to remove as much compound from it as possible. He scoops the excess into a bucket and later returns it to the storage area.

John moves to the extruder's head and uses a wrench to remove the four nuts holding the die and nipple against the faceplate. He grabs the tooling with heavily insulated gloves and sets it on a metal workbench. Then he loosens the bolt holding the heavy metal collar that secures the faceplate against the end of the barrel and bangs the collar apart with a heavy brass cylinder. The faceplate swings aside. Waves of smoke are drawn from the extruder into a ventilation duct.

Using his gloves, John grabs the end of the screw and slowly pulls it from the barrel. Periodically he stops and uses a pneumatically driven brush to clean it: Pull the screw a foot, buff, pull the screw, buff, and so on. When the heavy screw is almost out of the barrel, he grabs it like a barbell, pulls it free and carries it to a rack near the control panel. He attaches an extension to the wire brush and buffs out the barrel.

When the barrel is clean, John selects one of the eight screws from the rack. The screws are periodically measured for wear, and John installs one that the plant engineers have rated as somewhat worn. He explains that a slightly less efficient screw is better for the smaller gauge product he is running. The challenge is to apply a thin layer of insulation over the wire, and he accomplishes this partially by increasing the "line speed": the faster the speed, the thinner the layer of insulation. If the insulation is still too thick, he can decrease the RPMs of the extruder screw so that less compound is extruded. This reduces the frictional heat produced by the rotating screw and it may result in incompletely melted compound within the extruder barrel, a problem solved by increasing the temperatures of the barrel heaters. However, because the screw is now rotating slowly, the compound remains in the barrel longer exposed to higher heat and may degrade, resulting in a faulty product marred by black flecks.

John explains that the operators have learned that by allowing molten compound to leak back over the flight (i.e., helical ridge) of the slightly worn screw, the RPMs can be maintained sufficiently high to mix and melt the compound without an excessive amount exiting the tooling. If the screw is too worn, however, the leakage effects surges of compound that produce a pulsating outside diameter of the wire. Each screw has a changing reputation for performance on different gauges of wire and each operator has his favorites.

After inserting the screw into the barrel, John walks over to a computer terminal outside the Tool Control room in order to select the die and nipple he will install. He has already measured the outside diameter of the conductor with his micrometer and he enters the value into the terminal. The screen prompts him to enter the outside diameter of the finished wire as specified on the paperwork he received. Next he enters the outside diameter of the nipple he proposes to use, and the inside diameter of the proposed die. The latter two diameters are estimates based on his previous experience with similar gauge products. The computer calculates two values called "area draw" and "ratio" that must fall within specified ranges. These values express the relationship between the thickness of the compound as it emerges from the tooling and its thickness as hardened insulation on the finished wire.

The printout indicates an unacceptable area draw; he changes the nipple diameter and receives an acceptable value. John scans a list of available tooling and finds no nipple of that diameter. He chooses another that is close in diameter and enters it into the computer; the area draw and ratio remain within the acceptable range and he requests the nipple and die from Tool Control.

He remarks, "Sometimes you get it right away, but sometimes you have to play with the computer a while to get everything right." With familiar products and gauges he remembers acceptable tooling and thus performs no calculations.

I ask John to explain area draw and ratio, and his explanation differs slightly from those of other operators. In fact, even senior operators jokingly disagree when they try to explain the concepts, and they conclude that

I should ask an engineer for "the right explanation." John, like other operators, understands area draw and ratio as values that must fall within a specific range, and he also knows how changes in die and nipple sizes affect both values. He thus has a practical knowledge of tooling set-ups and their relationship to the values, but he was unable to explain the concepts of the two ratios or the causal relationships between tooling changes and ratios. His knowledge is focused on producing acceptable products rather than providing theoretical explanations for underlying processes and causes. Engineers concur that only a handful of operators possess theoretical understanding of the concepts, and they agree that the operators' practical knowledge is adequate for their tasks. One commented, "As long as the area draw and ratios are within this range [points to a diagram] the product is OK. The operators need to know how to get them into that range, but they don't need a textbook knowledge of how it's working."

The extruder has been shut down for twenty minutes when John returns to it. He places the old tooling under a pneumatic press mounted on the extruder and uses it to knock the die heater, die, and nipple apart. He fits the new tooling into the ringed die heater and secures the assembly with a bolt. He repositions the faceplate, fits the collar in place, and pounds the halves together with the brass cylinder. Then he attaches the new die heater/tooling assembly with four bolts.

John loads a new reel of conductor on the pay-off device and threads it through the pay-off dancer. He pronounces the conductor wire oily and ties a soft rag around it, anchoring a corner to the dancer with a piece of scrap wire. The rag will remove the excess oil as the wire is drawn through it. When I jokingly ask if the rag is specified, he laughs and says, "Just a trick we've learned. If the conductor is rough some guys will tie a wad of steel wool like that to smooth it, then the rag afterward to clean it."

After mixing several cups of colored chips ("color concentrate") into a large bucket of compound, he fills the hopper, turns on the screw, and sets the heaters to the temperature profile he prefers for this product. By the time he has opened his paperwork by entering data describing the materials he is using and the settings on the machine, the tooling is warm and melted compound is oozing from it. He adjusts the screw RPMs, double-checks the bank of thermostats, and then turns four bolts in the die heater to "center the flow" of compound. Finally, he threads the conductor through the nipple, ties it to the end of the old order, and starts the capstans.

During the observation-interview, John says that running the extruder is challenging because of the variety of products, many of which use compounds that are difficult to control. There are several hundred unique compounds, of which ten to fifteen are regularly used. Compounds may differ in melting temperatures, flow properties, the length of time they may remain in the barrel without degrading, and their sensitivity to changes in ambient air temperature and humidity.

Lester, an operator assigned to the adjacent extruder, wanders over and listens to our conversation. I comment that I have seen many machines running with no operator present, and ask both operators whether they watch their machines while they are running. They agree that the operator should remain near the machine except to retrieve materials from Storage, but some operators occasionally leave to talk with friends. John says it depends on the product being run and whether the operator is "comfortable with it," and Lester replies, "That's true, but you really shouldn't ever leave it for long. Best thing is to ask another guy to watch your machine."

As Lester talks, he feels the moving wire on John's machine every few minutes, and returns to his machine to do the same. He also glances at the cone of molten compound, looking at its length and shape. He sketches an ideal cone on a tablet, and says that he primarily monitors the cone and the "feel" of the wire. Occasionally he glances at the electronic micrometer gauge to ensure that the wire is within the specified diameter, but his attention is directed toward the wire speeding past him. He says that the micrometer reading fluctuates, and he only watches it for indication of a trend, such as a gradually increasing diameter. He holds up his manual micrometer and says, "This is what I trust. It never lies."

Every ten or fifteen minutes Lester scans several gauges that monitor the pressure within the barrel and the temperatures along it. Excessive pressure is hazardous and a discrepant thermostat reading may indicate a faulty heater that could affect the wire. His pattern of monitoring is thus twofold: He frequently monitors the product for quality, while he occasionally scans the control panel for discrepant readings. He explains that monitoring is complicated by the limitations of the extruder controls. For example, a discrepant thermometer reading may indicate a faulty heater or gauge. Thus, before adjusting the other heaters to compensate, he watches the product closely for the symptoms of altered temperatures. "An experienced operator will pick up those signs and make an adjustment before a rookie even notices, and when he does, he usually makes too many adjustments so you can't tell what's wrong."

Because the extrusion process is the most complex and unstable in the plant, problems are ubiquitous and troubleshooting is especially important. Operators utilize several sources of information to determine optimal set-ups and to solve the problems that invariably arise. Memory is especially important for veteran operators, and some also keep "black books" documenting their favorite set-ups and notes about the resulting product. Formerly, such notebooks were the primary reservoir of operator knowledge, and they were jealously guarded. Today, these notebooks are seldom maintained except by operators in training, having been replaced by the file of operator-created fact sheets documenting recommended set-ups and typical problems. Other operators are routinely asked for advice, and if the problem remains unsolved, a lead operator may coordinate troubleshooting.

The troubleshooting process begins with the recognition and categorization of fault; these in turn suggest corrective actions. For example, "drool" results from particles of molten compound that build up around the tooling being pulled off by the moving conductor to form irregularities in the insulation. "Chill" may occur if the conductor brushes against the tip. Improper or delayed cleaning of the barrel may result in streaky insulation.

According to operators, engineers, and supervisors, excellent troubleshooters such as Lester and John quickly detect symptoms of faults, recognize diverse types of faults and tactics to mitigate them, and then patiently await the results of their efforts. Above all, they monitor the product carefully and perform few adjustments, while the novice makes more adjustments so that quickly, according to Lester, "You can't tell what's causing what anymore. [If asked to help] I return all the settings to how I think the order should run and wait till the product stabilizes, then I make an adjustment and wait to see what happens."

The complex and concealed interactions of variables further complicates troubleshooting, for actions taken to correct one problem may effect new ones. Engineers and senior operators concur that the very best troubleshooters understand the operation of the machine and are able to visualize the pattern of interacting variables.

Lester, for example, notes that five process variables may be within acceptable limits, but the effect of any one differs depending on the values of the others. In effect, there are myriad constellations of values, only some of which may cause problems. He continues, "You have to understand how they all interact," although he believes that few operators do. Instead, most operators attend sequentially to the variables, making sure each is "in spec." Although this may be satisfactory for most problems, it is insufficient for solving the difficult problems that regularly arise.

John and Lester, and all the operators in this area, agree that the product specifications are primary, and the process specifications listed on fact sheets are secondary. "They're a starting point, really," says John. "You should follow them. Common sense says you should do what's worked before. But if the product isn't right you have to vary them." Thus, the nuances of style rest upon a foundation of variances in machines and materials which must be mitigated in order to produce an "in spec" (satisfactory) product.

Case Study: Cabling

We now move to the Cabling area to examine operator practices in an area performing a more stable process. A veteran operator, Ralph, has agreed to demonstrate operation of Cabler 10, a large machine that can twist up to thirty components together in a large cable. A cart loaded with dozens of spools of wire is positioned near the idle machine. Ralph checks the schedule posted on the cabler to verify that the spools on the cart are those to be loaded next. An envelope resting on the spools contains the production order, material list, material issue form, and the manufacturing specification form that Ralph will work from.

He studies a cross-sectional diagram of the cable in which each component wire is labeled with a number that corresponds to a legend below it. Ralph says he uses the diagram to visualize the completed cable so he can determine the sequence in which he will load spools of wire onto the cabler's axles (each mounted in a "bay"), for the 24-component construction is complex and costly. He comments, "There's a lot of pressure in Cabling because a cable this size is so costly. It's got hundreds of hours in it from other areas. You can't fuck it up." After studying the diagram, Ralph indicates that the varying diameters of the cable components will make it difficult to produce a round product.

He rolls the cart of spools closer and begins sorting them into stacks of identical material. Several of the individual spools hold insufficient wire for the cable, so Ralph will have to reload the machine with identical material during the run. Because this particular cable is quite complex, Ralph has received a "match sheet" specifying the order in which the spools of identical component wire should be loaded in order to minimize splices and produce the longest possible lengths of completed cable. Such match sheets are not provided with simpler cables; the operator must determine the sequence in which to load spools.

After sorting and stacking the spools of component wire, Ralph verifies that the paperwork "makes sense" and corresponds to the spools of wire on the cart. Using his micrometer, he measures and counts the strands of wire on each spool. He indicates a successful inspection on the quality checklist and then examines the manufacturing specifications for the crucial specifications: the length of the lay (the distance it takes for the cable to complete one spiral), the direction it must twist, and the outside diameter of the cable. The latter is especially important since a thick cable weighs more per foot, a critical factor in some applications.

Ralph notes the specified lay and looks at a chart on the machine that indicates the two gears recommended to produce it. He removes the gears from a nearby rack and, using a wrench, installs them in the machine's two gearboxes. Next he selects a die slightly larger than the specified outside diameter of the cable and attaches it to the die holder, which he adjusts to bring the component wires together. Between the bays and the die he installs a multihole disk ("spider"), which guides the wires from the rotating bays through the die.

His set-up in place, Ralph begins loading spools in twenty-four of the cabler's bays. The pattern of loading will determine the order of the component wires in the cable, and Ralph meticulously checks the spools against the cross-section diagram. At each bay, he removes its axle and places a spool of wire on it. He slips a metal collar over the axle and tightens it with a bolt, thereby securing the spool on the axle. Then he hoists each axle-spool assembly into its bay and fits a heavy leather strap over the axle.

He next adjusts the tension by turning a nut that cinches the leather strap against the axle, thereby preventing the spool from turning freely. This braking action creates the resistance that keeps the component wire taut as the machine runs, and it is imperative that the tension be appropriate for the component gauge (heavier gauges require more tension) and the weight of the spool (heavier spools require more tension). The relative tensions must be balanced too, so all twenty-four components pass smoothly through the die, resulting in a symmetrical product. "Getting the tensions right takes time. Too little tension and there's slack in the cable. It's loose. Too much and you stretch the conductor till it's out of spec."

As Ralph loads each bay, he pulls the component from the spool and inserts it through a hole in the spider, commenting that he has a mental pattern of how to thread the spider in order to effect the specified cross-section of cable. An hour later the bays are loaded, and the component wires are threaded through the spider and die. Ralph splices the bundle of components to the end of the previous cable and pulls it ahead by starting the tractor, which functions like the extruder's capstan to pull the product through the machine. Although the control panel is studded with knobs, buttons, and dials, he says he regularly uses the start and stop buttons, and the speed pot.

Ralph monitors the machine by scanning the rotating bays for emptying spools of component wire. Monitoring is more complicated when the operator applies a second layer of components around another completed cable, since he must watch for splices in the initial "core" cable and mark them with ink so they can be removed. Ralph stands on a well-worn patch of concrete eight feet from the control panel, and says, "This is my spot." From it he can see from behind the bay wheel to the take-up device and still be close enough to the control panel to shut the machine off if necessary.

As the end of his shift draws near, Ralph approaches the footage of cable produced on the schedule posted on the machine and initials it. The order is only partially complete, and soon another operator will take over the machine. Ralph stops the machine since the next operator has not appeared, and walks away to punch out and drive home.

Several minutes later, Bill arrives at the Cabler. He verifies the paperwork, making sure the machine is loaded with the correct material in the correct sequence, and then he examines Ralph's set-up, starting and stopping the machine several times. Finally, he comments, "I feel comfortable with it, but I wouldn't do it this way." Bill says the die is acceptable, but somewhat snug, and he worries that it may abrade the cable passing through it. "Here's the problem," he says, pointing to the spider. "I'd use a different spider here. [Gesturing with his hands] "The components should flow through the die smooth and natural. See, they're touching here." Bill suspects that Ralph installed a tight-fitting die to force the components together, when instead he should have set up the spider differently.

Bill calls the cable "awkward," since the varying component sizes make it difficult to effect a round product. He remarks that he would have loaded three additional bays with inert "filler rod," material that does not affect the cable's electrical properties but helps produce a smoother surface.

Bill inspects the cable and comments that the lay is short and barely within specifications. He examines the gearboxes and finds that the gears are those recommended, but says, "I'd change them, but they're okay. The product's 'in spec,' but I'm gonna watch the O.D. [outside diameter of the cable]." Finally, Bill says, "I'm comfortable with it," and starts the machine.

As the machine runs and the bay wheel, which is eight feet in diameter, revolves rapidly, Bill leans against the machine. He comments that the process is simple, but "You have to be systematic to set it up right. Mistakes cost a lot here." He periodically glances at the bay wheel, and I ask what he is looking for. "I got a spool that's almost empty," he says. The spools are a blur of different colors to me, and again I ask what he is looking for. "Is there a meter or an alarm telling you when it's empty?" He explains that an alarm will sound if the spool empties, "but then you've lost your set-up. The trick is to stop the machine just before a spool is empty. That's what

I'm doing: Watching that spool." He moves closer to the control panel and suddenly bangs the stop button. The machine slows and stops, and Bill points to one spool with only two "wraps" of wire remaining on it. "*That's* what I was watching," he says with a smile.

In summary, the cabling process is quite different from extrusion. It is not affected by environmental conditions, and few variables are manipulated. Furthermore, both process and product are easily visible and accessible to the operator, who can stop the machine to inspect the cable or rotate a pay-off spool to test the tension. Although the bay wheel rotates rapidly, the components are pulled off slowly so that an alert operator can detect mistakes before too much costly scrap product has been made. Product specifications, too, are relatively forgiving, since the specified outside diameter and lay define an allowable range that is usually met easily.

The very ease of meeting product specifications here and the ambiguities of "good feel" constitute conditions in which little training is required for operators to run simple orders, while also supporting the gradual honing of "feel" over years or decades, as exhibited by Bill's ability to see an emptying spool that was invisible to the anthropologist.

Operator Style

Our case studies of the Extruding and Cabling areas have attempted to explicate practice in those areas, but they are of course necessarily based on how specific operators run similar machines and orders. To the outside observer, all cases of running the machines in an area appear identical, and equally mysterious, and we have seen that at some level of description operators do talk about and perform basic tasks such as inspecting, setting up, and troubleshooting. But there are also notable differences in how operators within an area often perform these nominally identical tasks. These differences, as we shall see in Chapter 7, are consequential from the perspective of the new operator seeking to learn the basics so effortlessly discussed by his or her colleagues.

Understanding the similarities and differences in practice must be approached with care. Operators develop "styles" that they, their supervisors, and product engineers discuss. For example, Extruding operators, such as John and Lester, sometimes prefer different combinations of dies and nipples. They may adjust the overall length of the extruder's cooling trough, as well as its distance from the tooling; operators have calibrated their favorite positions with felt pen marks on some troughs. While some operators use a vacuum attachment to "suck back" an elongated cone of compound, others adamantly refuse, claiming it increases the risk of drool.

Style is also expressed in the choice of temperatures of the heaters melting the compound.

Operators critique elements of other styles, although direct comparisons among them are rare, for to do so would violate the sanctity of the operator's right to "comfort." Styles may be distinctive, resulting in products that meet minimal specifications, but that, according to some engineers and supervisors, retain the signature of the operator. Still, operators do not dwell in private worlds, each using the machine to produce wire and cable that is an idiosyncratic, personal statement. Operator styles consist of variations within the constraints imposed by machines and product specifications. These constraints are tangible and they must be addressed by the operator, but they only partially determine the actions the operator can take.

Calhoun's machines, such as those in Extruding and Cabling, have characteristics that affect the engagement of the operator with the machine (Neisser 1983). First, these machines are largely visible and accessible to the operator. The extruder performs a complex transformation and much is hidden within the barrel, yet even here operators routinely penetrate its workings when they install new set-ups and screws. The flow of compound, too, provides evidence that heaters are working and the screw is propelling the compound through the barrel. The cabling machine has even fewer surfaces to conceal its workings.

Machines in other areas are similar. Each Shielding machine, for example, is driven by a leather belt looped around a drive shaft that propels a dozen such machines. Each machine is engaged with a clutch lever, and speed is determined by a pulley the operator positions in line with the belt. The force is transmitted through several sets of exposed gears to the pay-off and take-up axles, and to the revolving carriers of bobbins. Everything is exposed to view, and the impression is one of motion.

Second, the machines make specific physical demands upon operators. The extruding machine is exemplary. The barrel screw may weigh in excess of one hundred pounds; the extruder head is extremely hot and many senior operators have burn marks on their wrists and forearms; and "cutting on the fly" requires a modicum of agility and coordination. Less dramatically, operators must exert strength to load and unload heavy reels, install gears and load bays, and pull clutch levers. Even a machine's configuration may constrain how the operator monitors it, as evidenced by Ralph's monitoring of the cabler.

Third, the operators' senses are engaged in particular ways. The spooling machine operator stares at the whirling traverse of her take-up spool looking for irregularities in color that indicate a faulty mark. The Marking operator scrutinizes the wire for an aesthetically pleasing, "cosmetic" mark and describes the torch heating it as having "a soft-looking flame." The extruder operator points to the cone of compound and asserts that it "looks fine—good shape and length."

In some departments, notably Packing, the sense of touch is paramount, as the operator feels every inch of wire and cable for faults. More commonly, operators speak of "the feel" as they set the tensions of pay-offs and take-ups. Although various tension meters have been employed over the years, few have proven satisfactory: The operator still pulls on parts or plucks the taut wire or cable to assess tensions.

Finally, most machines can be loaded, set up, and run in order to assess the quality of the resulting product. The operator may easily stop the cabler or shielder, closely watching the moving wire on a marking machine, or cut a sample in Extruding. She may then adjust one or more controls or install new tooling. Thus, the operator focuses attention on the product (rather than the machine), and she can see what is occurring and "play" with the machine to effect the desired outcome.

Unlike Kramden Computers, production work in Calhoun Wire and Cable can be described in terms of positions and motions. It is a tactile world, and subjective judgments of appearance and touch are consequential. And most important for learning, it is a world in which there are few surfaces to obscure either the workings of machines or the actions taken by other operators. Operators can learn from their machines and by watching other operators, activities which were of limited value in Kramden Computers. This visibility inherent in so much of Calhoun's production work provides the basis for much of the learning by new operators. It is a very different learning arena than that of Kramden Computers, where much work was invisible to observation and supervisors controlled their workers through ignorance.

Our exploration of Extruding and Cabling also suggests that operators spend considerable time managing variances at their machines. In fact, variances pose the major threat to producing satisfactory products, allowing a striking opportunity to innovate "tricks" and otherwise demonstrate prowess as an operator. Operators engage individual machines that may vary in performance during a run. In addition, nominally identical machines may perform somewhat differently. For example, operators claim that each shielding machine runs somewhat differently after being rebuilt repeatedly over the years.

Operators encounter diverse variances to manage. Some result from improper handling of acceptable wire or cable. Splices in material sent between areas may be incorrect, too large for subsequent processing, improperly marked with ink, or so weak that it breaks. Traverse controls on the take-up may be incorrectly set, so the wire fails to "pay off" smoothly, and snags or breaks. Alternatively, the operator may receive incorrect material to process. Wire may be the wrong color, gauge, or type for a specified cable. Material may also be "out of spec," such as faulty insulation exported from Extruding, an illegible mark on a wire, or a scraped cable. Products may be incorrectly routed through the plant, thereby omitting a step in processing. Faulty control gauges may result in poorly processed material, and operators may fail to set machine speeds or temperatures properly.

Finally, paperwork may be incorrect, and so operators carefully verify it before proceeding. Erroneous specifications occasionally arrive; numbers or units of measurement may be juxtaposed; data fields may not be completed; calculations may be erroneously computed; or discrepancies may arise between quantities, locations, or statuses of reels of products as indicated on the computerized inventory control system and the physical condition of the product.

Variance thus arrives from many sources, and a primary operator responsibility is its management: detecting and removing variances before they are exported from an area, developing acceptable accounts for the inevitable variances that do escape, and detecting imported variances before they damage machinery or are further processed. However, management of variance is actually not so straightforward, since interpreting its cause is often problematical, allocating responsibility is contentious, and regardless of the best efforts, faulty material and paperwork are routinely exported between areas. We will explore the larger implications of variance for learning in Chapter 7.

We have seen the interplay of machine characteristics, operator strategies, and variance in all areas of the production floor, such as Marking where some operators simultaneously run three marker machines. Wire to be processed is loaded onto the pay-off, strung through the dancer, and then, if a mark is being applied, is run through a pair of metal wheels, one of which applies the mark to the moving wire. The wire passes into an oven that bakes the ink onto the surface and then winds around a dancer and the take-up reel. Several optional heaters may also be used to heat the wire. Marks are specific as to color, size, message, spacing, and, more ambiguously, clarity.

Clair is setting up an order of wire for marking. She installs the three-inch-diameter metal wheel that will apply the mark and prepares her "wipe," the plastic plug that brushes the wheel and removes excess ink. Clair says she prefers a hard wipe over the softer ones preferred by some other operators. She uses a razor blade to trim the end to the angle she prefers; repeatedly, she cuts, examines, and cuts again. Then she fits the wipe in its holder, which she positions high against the wheel; other operators mount it lower.

The wire will pass between the marking wheel and a guide wheel, and Clair next adjusts the tension holding the wheels together. If the pressure is too light the wire may vibrate free, while excessive pressure forces the wheels into the wire, marring its surface. Clair says the marking wheel need only "kiss the wire" (lightly touch it). She explains that she has learned to get some otherwise recalcitrant products to "take the mark" by aligning the guide wheels so that the wire is pulled over the marking wheel at a slight angle. "I don't know why it works, but it does. Someone told me about it," she remarks. Clair also notes that some products are exceedingly difficult to mark and the operators have learned to mix two types of ink to effect the mark.

After stringing the wire through the machine and starting it, Clair wanders among her four machines, stirring the inkwells at each with a twist of wire to assess its viscosity. The heat of the machine can thicken the ink, and periodically she squirts a stream of solvent into a well and sloshes it around.

Clair periodically inspects the quality of the mark as the wire races by. She can only view it in a four-foot-long area between two pulleys and it is difficult to focus on the moving wire. She picks up a blank IBM card from a pile on the machine and holds it behind the wire as it leaves the first pulley. She presses the wire against the card with her thumbs and allows the moving wire to propel her fingers and the card. Shuffling her feet slightly to keep up with the moving card, she glances closely at it: The card creates a background for the mark that freezes it for viewing. She releases her grip before her fingers are pulled around the second pulley. Operators in other departments noted that they had been cross-trained in Marking and were comfortable with everything except "the IBM card thing." Standard now, the practice was invented by an operator.

Like operators throughout the plant, Clair had developed a style of running the machine that was both permitted and necessitated by the variances she encountered. Much of this style consists in variations in ways to perform the basics, but we also find Clair employing tricks, some of which are explicitly illicit. Such tricks are ubiquitous: the extruder operator's steel wool and rag tied around the conductor wire, and the weighing down of wire with an assemblage of washers so that it will not vibrate are representative. These tricks are often ingenious solutions to recurring problems, and most are invented by individual operators in the course of running orders.

The production floor is, however, not so much a place of creative innovators as it is a place of imitation and borrowing: The tricks are learned by watching and listening to other operators, and from instruction by operator-trainers.

Tricks are significant because they take us from officially sanctioned tasks and skills into a more ambiguous realm of production-floor expertise. While most tricks are permissible, others are clearly not. And the operator does not obtain them from books or training classes, but by becoming a member of the community of practice on the production floor.

The effects of variances are not always mitigated, and problems in production invariably arise. Operators develop strategies for diagnosing the causes of these problems and implementing solutions to them. These troubleshooting strategies also comprise an operator's style. The distinction between routine adjustments and troubleshooting is fuzzy, but operators in each area describe the troubleshooting tricks used to correct faults while running orders. We can explore troubleshooting by watching Edwin, a senior operator in Shielding.

The Shielding operator encounters several types of faults, such as gaps between strands of shielding wire or tangles of broken shielding wire ("bird nests") wrapped around the product. When confronted by any faulty wire, Edwin says that he first examines the size of the aperture in the guide in case the carrier wires have room to vibrate excessively before wrapping around the cable. Then he checks that all moving parts are freshly oiled, and he adjusts the small levers that effect fine adjustments in carrier tension. He demonstrates by adjusting a lever and then feeling the strand of wire.

Edwin starts a machine and watches it for several minutes. The carrier wire breaks and Edwin inspects the machine. He examines the aperture and rubs his finger over any metal surface that contacts the broken wire. "Nicks, tiny nicks can do it, this wire is so fine [thin]," he says. He pulls the clutch lever and the machine jerks to a start. The wire breaks and he disengages the clutch. This time he squints at the guide and again rubs the inside to detect nicks that might be snapping the wire. He also inspects the smooth metal bars that direct the thread-like carrier wire from the bobbins to the guide.

He engages the clutch, but the wire breaks after several minutes. Edwin removes the bobbin of broken wire and inspects its traverse for "crossovers" of wire that can snag; he judges the traverse "clean." Nevertheless, he sets the bobbin aside and installs a new one. He marks it with ink so if the wire again breaks he can immediately identify that position on the carrier wheel.

Again, the wire breaks. Edwin adjusts the tension lever and starts the machine. Fifteen minutes later it is still running smoothly, and he pronounces the cause of the breakage as "bad carrier wire."

Edwin's troubleshooting routine begins with an inspection of the machine set-up—tensions, pulleys, gears, oiling—and then proceeds through inspections for defective parts, which he has learned are associated with specific faults. He describes the work as a mixture of experience, common sense, and playing with the machine. While junior operators focus on tensions and obvious nicks, Edwin rubs his fingers over any surface the wire passes, commenting, "You just never know. I've seen nicks so tiny you can barely feel them, but they snag the wire." He also has tricks for handling other products. For example, he has learned from experience that one product that requires twelve bobbins of carrier wire runs without mishap on a sixteen-bobbin machine loaded with only twelve bobbins. Why this trick works remains unknown: "It shouldn't make a difference, but it does. Maybe it changes the speed slightly, but it works, and other guys do it, too."

Edwin is a virtuoso operator and his troubleshooting skills are highly regarded. Like other excellent troubleshooters, he determines that the set-up and loading are correct and then looks for obvious problems with the material or machine. Once the latter are running well, he narrows the search for causes through trial and error, effecting one remedy at a time. He claims his routine is based on his knowledge of machine functioning and a healthy awareness of its limits: "These are old machines, you know. They were invented to make shoelaces and we've adapted them for this. But you can't adjust them forever. Sometimes you just have to give up and move the order to a different machine." Although he searches for causes of faults, he points out that his primary goal is to get the order running, and he sometimes varies settings just to try something different. Edwin calls this "playing with the machine" and says it is often faster than a more systematic approach. Sometimes he plays with the machine and effects a cure without understanding the cause of the problem or why an action solved it. He also reports that playing has led to some of his troubleshooting tricks.

Because of the constraints imposed by the machine, experiences with common faults, and similarities in training, troubleshooting strategies are similar, but each operator's repertoire of strategies is somewhat different. Alice, another Shielding operator, says that she has memorized the problems that occur when she runs particular products, and although she follows a troubleshooting strategy she does not follow it methodically: "I try changing things real fast if there's a problem. I switch machines, I switch bobbins, I oil everything. I know the products that cause problems, and I won't spend too much time on troubleshooting them. I just change something." Jason, a third operator, has memorized countless machine-product pairings and how nominally identical machines must be adjusted differently to run the same product. "Look at this," he says. "Look where this die is positioned. Now look at this machine." The die is positioned at least an inch higher. "They're running the same product, they're the same machines. But you just have to run this one with the die higher. No one knows why, but you do and you get good product—until they rebuild it [laughter]."

These operators provided clear and explicit accounts of their troubleshooting strategies; each had reputations for being helpful trainers. Other operators had difficulty in clearly explaining their routines because they were taken for granted. Several operators steadfastly maintained that the work was easy and troubleshooting was merely the exercise of common sense. One commented, "I don't know. I just look the machine over and adjust anything that needs it. It's easy after a while [pause]; I don't know what I do [laughter]." Even Edwin mentioned that he inspected the position of one guide only after my questioning; second nature motivated the action.

We may conclude then that operators may vary not only in their repertoires of troubleshooting tricks, but also in their awareness of them and their abilities to explain them. This, of course, has implications for training and learning on the production floor. Like other elements of operator style, troubleshooting tricks may be shared, but they are not systematically compared. Accordingly, some operators are widely recognized as ones who can and will assist others, while others are seldom asked for help. Edwin commented that some operators who consider themselves to be good troubleshooters still rely on the expertise of others in extraordinary cases. "Yeah, and you know we choose our orders from the queue. You're supposed to take it based on the 'hot list' [priority orders] and how long a reel has been sitting there, but some guys will look it over and leave something they have trouble running. If you ask them, they'll say their machine was already set up for the product they took. They troubleshoot by avoiding trouble." Or in Extruding, many junior operators claim they know "everything" needed to run orders, and if they run into problems they hail Lester or another "key" (virtuoso) operator: "I've been here two years and finally feel pretty comfortable out here. I can handle everything they throw at me, and if I have a problem I can get Federico or Lonnie to help out."

Conclusion

The production floor described in this chapter is much different from that described in the previous chapter. The former is one of unambiguous tasks, formal procedures, and work that is simple and predictable. In this chapter, we see variance lurking as a constant threat to "making product." It provides both the need for the strategies to mitigate its effects and the opportunity for operators to develop slightly divergent styles.

Previously, operators described their work in terms of basic tasks and skills, and their accounts ignored the particular characteristics of machines or products. In this chapter, we have seen that effective operators are sensitive to the idiosyncrasies of machines, the characteristics of products, and the ubiquitous threat of paperwork errors. If their accounts of their work are thin, it is only because they take so much of what they do for granted. And if they make their work look easy, it is not because they apply a set of previously internalized abstract principles, but rather because they are sensitive to slight variances and are equipped with large repertoires of troubleshooting tricks that they rapidly employ.

Operators develop slightly different styles of operating the machines, and although their styles of set-ups, tricks, and troubleshooting strategies are widely discussed they are not systematically compared. Operators assess each other as sources of assistance, and they assess the merits of various strategies, but they do not delve too deeply, for that would violate the operator's right to be comfortable. Thus, the production floor is the site of abundant strategies, and a challenge for the new operator to make sense out of the diverse, often contradictory advice he or she receives.

Rather than learning the basics as a set of unambiguous skills and then developing personal variations of them later, operators are exposed to variations in style from the outset. The basics are better viewed as inevitable tasks to be performed, not as unique ways to perform them. Likewise, the operator is not simply someone who internalizes and then applies procedural knowledge, but rather she confronts practical problems that are solved by innovation, borrowing, or friends. Above all, we have seen a world in which mastery of technical skills accompanies and is made possible by gradually increasing participation in a community of practice.

Despite this richer view of work, our view is still narrowly focused on the operator performing traditional tasks. Yet the work of the operator has changed dramatically in the past few years, and a narrow focus on machines is now insufficient. Specifically, operators in Calhoun have been thrust into the role of information processors in order to improve the production process, and they are expected to assume responsibilities in producing the workplace itself rather than just "making product." We discuss these changes in Chapter 6.

Our view here is also narrow in that it assumes we can understand the operator's work by observing operators *at* work and can discuss that work with them. But larger systems shape the operator's work at Calhoun Wire and Cable, and we must explore these as well. Specifically, operators are affected by the system of feedback about the results of strategies that affect work, and by the production-floor culture with its associated meanings. We turn to this topic in Chapter 7.

6   COMPETITION, PAPERWORK, AND PROJECTS

Basically, the work here is the same as always: Wire is wire! But it's changed, too. There's a lot of paperwork now and participation, which is good and bad. They will listen now and you can have ideas and instead of being told they're dumb they say, "Let's try it." It's like "put up or shut up." Now you're expected to participate so you can see your ideas make a difference.

—Extruding operator

Sometimes I just want to do my job.

—Another Extruding operator

The tasks of Calhoun's machine operators have always revolved around the direct labor of producing wire and cable. Indeed, operators with decades of experience told tales of both continuity and change. While operators continued to be assigned to machines that they operated within the constraints imposed by supervisors and engineers, new products, processes, and machinery simultaneously modified their work. This pattern of gradual change ended abruptly during the 1980s as the global market for specialty wire and cable products became increasingly competitive, and Calhoun's management struggled to adjust. As a result, operators assumed new responsibilities, and production work was transformed as new tasks were grafted onto existing ones.

In this chapter we explore production work in an era when operator participation has been solicited, even demanded, by management. We begin by reviewing management's response to the new market conditions and how it affected tasks on the production floor. Then we discuss the function of data collection in improving the company's competitiveness, and how this has resulted in an explosion of paperwork to be handled by the operators.

The latter have became processors of information as well as of wire and cable. We turn next to the involvement of operators in projects intended to improve the production process. In this way, production work is no longer exclusively labor involved in "making product," but rather operators making the workplace in which wires and cables are produced.

MANAGERIAL RESPONSES

Techno Corporation has a tradition of performing basic scientific research that results in new, patented products. Calhoun Wire and Cable had enjoyed decades of success in marketing products for specialized applications due to its ability to produce wire and cable that met highly specific and idiosyncratic specifications, and by virtue of the protection provided by patented products that had become world standards.

The earlier market had several implications for the production floor. Because of the absence of competitive pressures, customers had few alternatives but to accept Calhoun's product on its own terms; orders were sometimes overdue and quality occasionally varied. There were few incentives to control costs of production, especially the amount of scrap wire and cable.

All this changed during the 1980s, when several patents expired and foreign competitors, especially Japanese manufacturers, moved into the specialty wire and cable market. Calhoun's management adapted to the new market conditions through several strategies, each of which affected life on the production floor.

First, management attempted to reduce costs by reducing the scrap produced at each step of production. To do so, the company intensified its data collection activities on the production floor, and operators were required to record data concerning the time spent "in an order," the materials used, the conditions under which the product was processed, and the properties of the finished product. Most areas developed quality checklists in order to guide the operator through the handling of an order.

Second, the company sought to improve the timeliness of its deliveries to customers. PRODCON, a computerized scheduling and production control system, replaced an existing pencil-and-paper system for tracking production. PRODCON's computer terminals appeared in each department, although only a few operators in each used them. PRODCON did, however, generate the extensive paperwork that accompanies an order throughout its processing. We will discuss PRODCON further in Chapter 8.

Third, Calhoun's sales representatives successfully marketed the company's ability to meet customer requests for unique products. The company could produce approximately 24,000 distinct products, although far fewer were produced in any year. This expanded number of products increased the product specifications and process settings operators encountered. The company also marketed its capability to trace the conditions under which any piece of wire or cable was produced. This was especially desirable for customers who used Calhoun's products in applications where failure could be catastrophic, such as in aircraft or weapons systems. This, too, required extensive data collection by operators.

Finally, production management and engineering intensified their efforts to stabilize the processes for producing many products, thereby reducing the variances endemic on the production floor. A new production manager believed that vital knowledge had been disseminated among the operators who for years had cajoled their machines into processing troublesome products. Accordingly, management launched a broad effort to obtain cooperation in improving the production process via intensive data collection, adoption of some statistical process control methods, and involvement in a variety of projects.

Management's attempts at adaptation had two very broad effects on the work of operators. First, the operators' burden of paperwork increased dramatically. Each order today is typically accompanied by a thick packet of documents containing detailed information about the product and how it should be processed, and the prudent operator carefully examines each page in order to verify the accuracy and consistency of data. The operator must also record extensive data on the various quality checklists and "cost center reports" used in each area, thereby increasing the importance of thorough, accurate data entry. Correct handling of paperwork also entails considerable background knowledge by operators, who must know what to look for on the documents they receive, how to perform any required measurements, how to perform specific calculations, and how to enter data in the correct fields of a form.

Second, work on projects as a component of the operators' job descriptions altered both the tasks performed by operators and their involvement in the company's long-term fortunes. Successful projects often involved producing brief written reports, speaking in public forums such as area meetings or "brainstorm sessions," determining the costs and benefits of alternative interventions, and, more generally, viewing the production floor as a social and technological system that can be changed following experimentation. These activities were very different from those associated with running machines. Less obviously, projects involved the operators in producing the workplace in which they worked, and thereby they assumed the operator's continued involvement in the fate of the company. Projects have thus affected the nature of work on the production floor and the relationship of operators to their employer.

These changes in operator responsibilities altered production work, and not all operators adapted to the new regime: Some were terminated, others voluntarily departed. Nevertheless, we should not exaggerate the discontinuity in production-floor life. Operators had long handled paperwork, taken measurements, and generated informal procedures for handling recalcitrant products. And some operators had always collaborated with engineers and supervisors in special projects. What changed were the relative importance of these information-processing and workplace-building activities, and their inclusion in the operator's job description.

Packing Department and Paperwork

We now turn our attention to the impact of paperwork on one production department. Packing Department is called the hub of the production floor since products in various stages of completion pass through it, often routed from different areas of the plant. Operators here are the intermediaries between the plant and customer, and their decisions about the quality of product and knowledge of diverse customer specifications are critical. Because of its central position, Packing is the preferred entry portal for new workers, and thus it directs considerable resources to training.

The spooling machine holds a large pay-off reel of wire or cable, and a smaller take-up spool which holds the product the operator "spools to the order." The operator loads a pay-off reel and strings it through a dancer, a sparker, and then up to the take-up spool. A small built-in desk with a calculator resting on it completes the spooling machine.

The operator sits on a stool lightly gripping the moving wire or cable between her fingers, guiding the product back and forth across the take-up spool traverse. As faults pass through the sparker, the alarm sounds, causing the operator to release her grip on the product and stop the machine by releasing a foot pedal. She removes the faulty section with wire cutters, splices the ends together, and then continues spooling the order. Inspection is essentially tactile and visual, as every inch of moving product is lightly felt by the operator, and the take-up traverse is watched for subtle differences in shading that might indicate a faulty mark or stripe.

We begin by observing Marta, a senior operator, as she spools an order. She holds up the transparent plastic envelope that contains the documents that specify how the cable should be handled. These documents— material list, production order, packing information form, material issue form, and various pregummed and printed labels—are Marta's primary sources of information. Other paperwork consists of the several blank forms that Marta will complete while she processes the order: the Packing cost center report, spooling-length distribution sheet, Packing quality checklist, and adhesive "length stickers" for each spool she fills with wire.

Marta lays out the paperwork on her machine's desk. In addition to the standard documents, she receives a copy of the Extruding cost center report prepared by the extruder operator who produced the wire, and a short primary wire identification tag containing information entered by other operators who handled the product. She separates the material issue form, material list, production order, packing information form, and the pregummed labels in order to verify the information they contain.

Marta cross-checks the coded identification numbers on the paperwork for consistency, as she says, "to be sure they make sense." For example, the uppermost line of the material list specifies the quantity of the product to be spooled, while the lower lines specify the amount of wire she has received. Since material is lost when she removes faults from the wire, the quantity printed on the lower lines must exceed that on the upper. She then transcribes information from the documents she has received to the several blank forms she will complete as she spools the order. Juxtaposing digits is a common error, and she cautions, "You have to be careful and methodical doing this, and have clear handwriting."

A handwritten number atop the material list tells her how much to spool; at the bottom, Marta finds the lot number of the pay-off reel from which the wire is to be spooled. She cross-checks it with the Material Issue Form to determine that she has all the reels allocated to the order and that the lot numbers match. Then she examines the production order for the code number identifying the type of operation she will perform, and comments that while it is usually the same for this particular product, it sometimes varies.

When she is satisfied that her paperwork is complete, the specifications are consistent and sensible, and the pay-off reel is correct, she "opens her paperwork" and prepares to inspect the wire by measuring its diameter, counting the individual strands of wire that comprise the conductor, and measuring a single strand of conductor. She enters the results on the Packing quality checklist she has prepared for the order. Marta scans the packing information form for the put-up: the size and color of take-up spools to be used, the type of splice she must use to connect the lengths of wire placed on the spool, the minimum footage of wire that the customer will accept ("good lengths"), the number of good lengths per spool, total footage of wire allowed per spool, and even the color of ink she must use to highlight the splices she makes.

Marta next prepares the two-page Packing quality checklist she will complete with the order. She places check marks in a column of boxes to acknowledge that she has verified the paperwork and read the put-up. Then she confirms that the pay-off reels and empty take-up spools are present. She completes the "quality check" section of the form after inspecting the wire and performing several tests specified by the customer. The remainder of the checklist reminds her to perform continuous quality checks, and reviews the criteria for satisfactory orders and proper distribution of paperwork. She rapidly places check marks in the appropriate boxes. Marta looks up and smiles, "Lot's of paperwork, huh? And I'm not even 'into' spooling the order yet!" I ask how she remembers how to handle all the paperwork and she replies, "My routine. I have a routine that I follow on every order."

Marta now prepares the Packing cost center report that will be used to determine the labor costs of production. Marta applies one of the pre-gummed labels to the first section of the report. She will complete this section of the form when she has finished spooling the order. For each order she records the total "good footage" spooled to it (i.e., the total footage of all lengths of wire shipped to the customer) and any unspooled wire remaining on the pay-off reel. She also records the amount of wire scrapped while spooling the order, the total footage of "shorts" (i.e., lengths of wire that are acceptable but shorter than the customer specified), and the amount of any questionable material sent to the plant's material review board for disposition.

Marta must also calculate the time spent completing the order. First she records the minutes spent stringing up the wire, opening the paperwork, asking questions, searching for missing reels, and so forth. If she encounters production-related problems while spooling the order she adds this "downtime" to her initial set-up time. She also records time spent on breaks, meetings, special projects, and personal activities. Upon finishing the order, she will record her time "out of the order" (i.e., the clock time when she completes running the order). Later, she will calculate the time spent processing the order.

After about twenty minutes of reviewing paperwork and inspecting product, Marta strings up the pay-off wire through the dancer and sparker to an empty take-up spool she has loaded onto her machine. She then places a gummed label on a blank Packing length distribution sheet in order to record the footage and quality of each length of wire she takes off the pay-off reel. She enters 12,000 feet in her electronic calculator, the total footage of wire that is allowed on the take-up spool.

Marta sits at the machine and presses the throttle pedal; the wire begins to run from the pay-off reel to the take-up spool. She grips the wire lightly in her right hand, constantly feeling it for faults and guiding it back and forth onto the take-up traverse. After several minutes, a fault triggers the sparker alarm and Marta releases the throttle. She reverses the spooling machine and runs it back and forth until she isolates the fault at the sparker.

Marta cuts the wire and notes the reading on the machine's counter: 1,137 feet, well over the 1,000-foot minimum length specified by the customer. She records that the first length taken off the pay-off reel is 1,137 feet of good footage on the Packing length distribution sheet. Then she enters the same value on the first line of the length sticker that she will affix to the spool's flange when it is full of wire.

Marta subtracts 1,137 from the 12,000 entered previously in the calculator; the resulting 10,863 indicates the remaining space on the take-up spool. After resetting the machine's footage counter to zero, Marta removes about 10 feet of wire around the fault and splices the good ends together. She records the 10 feet of scrap on the Packing length distribution sheet as the second length taken off the reel.

Marta resets the footage counter and begins spooling. As the counter registers 785 feet, she stops the machine, saying that the wire feels lumpy. She proceeds slowly, still complaining about the lumps. After spooling over 100 feet of wire, the lumps vanish, and she reverses the machine and returns to where they began. I feel the wire, but am unable to distinguish between good and lumpy wire. Marta notes the footage on the counter (785 feet) and returns to the Packing length distribution sheet, where she records the third length off the pay-off reel as 785 feet of good wire, followed by a fourth 110-foot length she calls "lumpy scrap." In addition, she places an asterisk by the third length, noting that it is good wire, but less than the minimum length. Marta removes a total of 895 feet of wire that cannot be spooled to the order, splices the wire from the pay-off reel to the last length on the take-up spool, and continues spooling.

Splices and faults trigger alarms all morning, and Marta occasionally complains about lumpy or rough wire. When the order is complete, Marta has taken sixty-three lengths of good and scrap wire off the pay-off, completed several Packing length distribution sheets, and asked another operator for a second opinion regarding some wire. At 11:20 A.M. she closes the order, noting this on the quality checklist. Using her calculator, she totals the values on the Packing length distribution sheet that she will enter on the Packing cost center report. She verifies that she spooled the correct amount of wire and that the amount removed from the pay-off reel is accurately recorded. Finally, she double-checks that each of the twenty-two spools she has filled have the correct labels and that each has a single length sticker recording the footage of each length of wire on the spool. The order complete, Marta departs for lunch.

Marta's morning of spooling is typical of the spooling operator's work, and it reveals the complexity of managing extensive paperwork. Her use of a routine is especially striking, and although all successful operators develop such routines, they differ in details. Marta's routine begins when she arranges the documents in order to determine that the requisite paperwork is present. Only after systematically cross-checking documents for consistency does she inspect the reel of wire or cable to be spooled, "get into" the paperwork, and ultimately commence spooling.

Marta's routine may be decomposed into smaller cycles in which she alternates between spooling wire, performing calculations, and entering information on her Packing length distribution sheet. In fact, she says that these subroutines are essential if she is to keep place in the order when confronted by periodic interruptions. For example, when a lead operator asked her a brief question, Marta answered immediately. However, when another operator asked her to confirm his assessment of some wire, she nodded silently and continued spooling until she found a fault that she noted on the Packing length distribution sheet. Only after subtracting it from the calculator total did she leave her machine.

In addition to stimulating the development of routines, the increase in paperwork has also created additional tasks for operators. For example, operators previously received scant paperwork and generally accepted as correct the information it contained, although they sometimes "caught" errors. With increasing paperwork has come an increased probability of error, and increased responsibility for verification. Minimally, this entails cross-checking values for discrepancies. Here the operator need know only which values on which documents should be consistent, something that even tyros are expected to perform. In the extreme, an entire document may be incorrect; more typically, only a pair of nominally identical numbers may differ. Other discrepancies are subtler, as when one pair of digits in a lengthy code are juxtaposed. Marta also reviews the units of measurement on each document, explaining, "I know some are in feet and others are in pounds."

Most of all, Marta verifies that the paperwork makes sense. This requires familiarity with the larger context in which orders are processed, and it is not directly apparent from examining the paperwork. Ivan, another spooler, recounts how he caught a subtle error. All the values on the paperwork he had received were consistent, but he recalled that he had handled the same product several months earlier. This time the specified put-up was different from the one he used before, but Ivan could not remember receiving an updated procedure, nor had the product been mentioned in any departmental meetings. He reported his concerns to a supervisor who used PRODCON to "pull up" the specifications, and they found that a clerical error had been made when the specifications were rewritten. Ivan said he would not be blamed if he had simply proceeded to put up the order as specified, but he confided, "It felt good to catch an error."

The importance of making sense is not confined to the Packing Department. While running a printing machine in Marking, Anand received paperwork instructing him to apply a five-digit code to a two-inch diameter cable. Although the specified print was less than $1/8$ inch high, Anand dutifully applied it. However, an error in typing the specifications had been made by a newly hired clerk and the mark was one specified for a smaller wire within the cable. Anand was reprimanded for following the specification because, as a coworker opined, "It doesn't make sense to put a tiny mark like that on a large cable. We never do it." In this case the operator failed to detect an error in seemingly correct information, and other operators agreed that Anand should have caught the error.

Handling paperwork, like running machines, is subject to differences in style. For example, in completing the quality checklist, Marta methodically enters data, item by item. Other operators develop slightly different strategies for utilizing the checklist. Sonia, another spooler, explains that, for many operators, the checklist is "just something else to do"; completing it item by item adds considerable time to the order. She taps her head with a finger and says she follows a routine that is "up here." It guides her verifications and inspections, but she waits until completing the order before entering data on the quality checklist. Then, in a flurry of check marks, she checks off each item and thereby confirms the quality of the order. Sonia explains that because of her routine she *knows* that if she has completed an order she performed all the operations on the checklist, and it is by definition acceptable.

Sonia's rationale for her strategy is that although the quality checklist is intended to simplify handling paperwork, it unnecessarily complicates her work. She simplifies her spooling by effectively making all-inclusive check marks upon completing the order. Operators use other simplifying strategies as well. Many reportedly see only that portion of a coded number that pertains to their immediate task, having learned to ignore the rest. Other operators recounted that they learned the errors associated with products and looked only for those errors. Products and paperwork with error-free histories received only a perfunctory verification. Some operators eliminated the need to calculate their time spent on an order by entering a standard value on their cost center reports, such as twenty minutes for set-up time. Only if the time spent was unusually divergent did the operator attempt to actually calculate the minutes.

Differences in spooling styles illustrate the complex effects that the paperwork burden places upon Packing operators. Attentiveness, memorization, and systematic work habits have been emphasized and are formally required. While most veteran operators develop these, the use of simplifying strategies indicates their limitations. Few such strategies are approved, and learning which ones can be implemented with little risk to the operator's job and which are forbidden is critical. The safety of a strategy is generally assumed until an error of omission or commission occurs, a supervisor is informed, and the operator is told about the mistake. Even then, the operator (or her supervisor) must establish a causal relationship between the strategy and an outcome, a task made difficult by the passage of time.

A related issue is the relative efficacy of different practices. Supervisors agree that operators who fail to develop clear routines make excessive mistakes, although they allow that various routines are possible. However, different practices may result in different outcomes, although they are deemed merely matters of style and subject to the operator's discretion.

Use of the calculator to compute the footage on a spool is illustrative. Marta's practice is first to enter the spool capacity (e.g., 12,000 feet) and then to deduct the footage of each good length as she spools it on. Other operators employ a different practice: They set the calculator to zero and then add the footage of each good length as it is spooled, stopping only at the spool's capacity. However, the two styles of computing footage are associated with different outcomes.

In Marta's subtraction method, she must cut the wire coming off the pay-off reel at 12,000 feet, even if the length is good. Of course, if the space remaining on a take-up spool is less than the minimum length specified for the order, she is forced to close that spool. The order will thus consist of many filled-to-capacity spools, along with a few spools with insufficient space for another minimal length of product.

In the second method, the operator continues to spool wire onto the take-up spool until either it reaches capacity or she decides to close the spool. For example, Lynn is spooling minimum lengths of 1,000 feet onto a 12,000-foot capacity take-up spool. She has observed that the good lengths are averaging nearly 2,000 feet; the longest possible lengths greatly exceed the acceptable minimum. With four lengths of wire on the take-up spool, Lynn cuts the wire to remove a fault. There is room for another 1,510 feet of wire, but Lynn dislikes cutting a good length of wire, so she "closes the spool" and begins a new one. When the first length runs to 2,378 feet she smiles and remarks that it was a good decision. The spools in her completed order will differ widely in the footage each contains, although she will have made fewer unnecessary cuts and thus provided the customer with the longest possible lengths.

Operators develop preferences for the subtraction or addition methods, and these become part of their style. While neither technique is intrinsically more mistake-prone, each effects differences in where good wire is cut, and accordingly both are not equally efficacious. Still, they are deemed alternative styles with which different operators feel comfortable.

To summarize, the proliferation of paperwork has had complex effects on the work of operators, Packing operators in particular. They are held accountable for verifying paperwork and inspecting the products they process, and thus their decision-making activities have significantly increased. Still, most of these decisions are routine. For operators such as Marta, decision making is less prominent than her use of memory and her disciplined, methodical handling of documents. Such traditional skills as paying attention, following instructions, and legible handwriting are critical to success.

Packing Department initially presents itself as a domain of algorithmic, shared procedures, but, as we have seen, this view is partial at best. The very abundance of information is overwhelming, and even aids like written checklists and procedures are of limited use. The importance of oral communication and the social nature of competence are vividly displayed, as when operators converge on a colleague who is spooling an uncommon or new product, or when they consult in small ways throughout their shift. Again, the relationships between formalized procedures and work practices are complex, and individual styles of handling paperwork persist. And new workers still confront an often bewildering array of styles from which they must create one of their own.

From Tinkering to Projects

Management's adaptation to new market conditions also resulted in support for a variety of projects in which operators were expected to participate. Such projects were operator- or management-initiated, and they focused upon the exigencies of running orders or a host of other concerns, such as noise abatement or workplace safety. Participation could be solitary, as when an operator became the "champion" of a cause, or collective, such as participation in Cabling team meetings. Some projects were ongoing, nearly institutionalized activities, while others were episodic, as when an operator was invited to join the team of engineers assessing a new machine.

Projects are significant in that they represent a discontinuity with the operator's traditional responsibility for running machines. Rather than working on the product, operators work on the workplace per se. Projects represent an innovation in the operator's job description, but they are deeply rooted in a tradition of "tinkering."

In order to understand tinkering, we must revisit the world of making wire and cable described in Chapter 5. There we saw that variances in machine performance and raw materials resulted in ubiquitous troubleshooting activities. Operators also developed tricks in order to cajole troublesome products through the machines. Tinkering represents an extension of tricks, although the distinction between them is often blurred. If tricks constitute temporary adjustments to a machine as it processes an order, by tinkering the operator permanently alters the machine in order to improve its performance or ease of operation (hopefully). Parts might be bent, welded on, ground off, repositioned by helpful maintenance workers, or alarms might be disabled so as not to draw attention to an inattentive operator.

Tinkering is a testament to operator ingenuity, but it has a more specific importance to us: It represents, albeit in frequently contraindicated ways, participation and commitment from the perspective of the operator. In this sense, there is a direct linkage between tricks, tinkering, and the required participation in formalized projects favored today by Calhoun's management.

Shielding area is the home of many successful tinkerers, such as Raul, an operator with six years' experience. While discussing how he monitors the eleven machines he is running, he points to one and says that the component wires of the cable are separating slightly, thereby creating a loose protective sheath over it. He examines the machine and then proclaims that the cable needs more tension to hold the components tightly together. The problem is that the cable tension cannot be adjusted on the machine.

Raul retrieves a brake the operators designed and had welded together by the Maintenance Department. It consists of a three-foot-long piece of channel-shaped iron with a peg projecting from one end, and a foot-long piece of iron rod welded to the other end, forming a tee. He positions the device so that the tee end is jammed into the machine and the channel rests on the rim of the pay-off reel. Then he stacks excess gears onto the peg until their weight presses the channel iron onto the rim with enough force to slow it. The slack vanishes from the cable instantly.

Such tinkering occurs in all areas of the production floor, and occasionally tinkering has been extended from machines to modifying processes.

Wayne is a highly regarded senior extruder operator who successfully tinkered with the production process. In telling the story, he points to an extruder running a very large cable onto a five-foot-diameter take-up reel and says they formerly used three-foot reels "because that was the way it was done." From his perspective, this was troublesome since the large diameter cable rapidly filled the reel, requiring him to frequently load new take-up reels. This also resulted in excessive splices between the lengths of cable on different reels, thereby weakening the product and causing it to break in other areas of the production floor.

Wayne followed an order of this product through the plant, asking friends in other departments for help in locating it, and found that it passed through a machine in the Marking area with a pay-off reel capacity of three feet. The next time an order for the product arrived, he refused to use the three-foot reels. When confronted by his supervisor, he explained that the procedure caused excessive splices, shorter lengths, and "had no quality basis." He accompanied the supervisor to the critical marking machine and suggested that the department be asked to justify using a three-foot pay-off reel. Soon thereafter, a larger pay-off reel was installed, allowing the extruder operator to use a larger reel.

In addition to authorized tinkering, unauthorized tinkering occurs as well. Pointing to a cabling machine, an operator says, "There's a part that's supposed to be there [touching a part of the machine], but if I want the machine to work right I have to take it off." Or a new machine is installed and within a day its annoying fault signal is disabled. Another operator persuades a maintenance worker to weld a new guide bracket onto a machine during the graveyard shift, when supervisors and engineers are seldom encountered.

Tinkering is a heterogeneous category of actions, but it represents, albeit in restricted form, the generation of workplace context by operators. Tinkerers effectively change machines, and operators function in a world that is not made entirely independently of their actions. The workplace is not merely a stage upon which skills are required and exercised, but rather the stage itself is built with the assistance of operators.

Tinkering, however, is viewed ambivalently by managers and engineers. On the one hand, it is desired since it represents the operators' commitment to meeting manufacturing deadlines. Engineers freely acknowledge that tricks and tinkering have been essential to controlling variances throughout the plant's history, although they formally prohibit unauthorized modifications to machines.

On the other hand, not all tinkerers are equally competent, and several machines have been rendered inoperable because of excessive tinkering.

Subtler is the effect on learning in the workplace: Tinkering conceals the true conditions under which a product is run, thereby making it difficult to correlate operator actions with outcomes. Specifically, a machine may be set up identically on several different occasions and produce a slightly different result each time because of the effects of unrecognized tinkering by the operators. In this way, local problem solving can obscure the foundations upon which action is taken, a theme to which we will return later.

Projects can be viewed as management's attempt to capture the benefits of the operators' often ingenious solutions to problems while simultaneously eliminating the costs that accompany them. This is of particular concern when Calhoun purchases new and costly machinery. Ironically, management generally views projects as distinct from (and opposed to) tinkering, while operators comment on the similarities between them.

Some examples of projects illustrate their scope. Brief classes are occasionally offered by operators; topics include safety issues and proper performance of some tasks. One or more operators may develop training manuals, procedures, and troubleshooting guides, or they may be temporarily assigned to another department in order to learn its tasks. Operators may also investigate some facet of the production process, such as the causes of downtime during a shift. Finally, they may develop solutions to production floor problems. For example, Extruding operators developed shields that fit around the extruder head to conserve heat and special die heaters that can easily be replaced. These projects clearly trace their ancestry to tinkering.

The development of electrotrude tooling by Wayne, an Extruding area operator, is the most elaborate operator-initiated project, and we will explore it in depth. Electrotrude tooling was developed to solve the recurring problems operators encountered while they extruded smaller gauges of some wires. Operators and engineers had long focused on adjustments to the standard extruder tooling. Die and nipple sizes, temperature settings, and line speed had all been adjusted without success, and operators were frustrated at the delays in running their orders. Product engineers lamented the variations in product quality and the seemingly endless effort devoted to a handful of products, while management was concerned that only a few virtuoso operators could run the products.

Wayne began "playing" with the tooling by trying different combinations of die and nipple diameters, hoping for one that would ameliorate the problem. In addition, he varied the positions of the nipple by moving it in and out of the die. Although this conformed to what Wayne visualized as a solution, repositioning the nipple was only partially successful. After exhausting the permutations of tooling diameters and adjustments, he asked a different question: What tooling design would allow him to run the trouble-some products?

Wayne's innovation is a tooling design that allows the operator to change a critical parameter of the tooling by repositioning the nipple. Wayne had also learned from experience that changing this parameter could minimize drool. Thus, he hoped that his idea would solve several chronic problems.

Wayne drew sketches of his proposed tooling at home and showed them to fellow operators and supervisors, but the response was unen-couraging. He recalls, "It was the usual: It won't work." Although few people understood his innovation, those who did pointed out problems Wayne had not anticipated. "I worked on them mentally," constantly weighing the ad-vantages and disadvantages of each idea.

Wayne again explained the innovation to his supervisor, who encour-aged him to pursue it. He enlisted the help of a friendly engineering techni-cian and together they modified some tooling in order to fashion a prototype. Wayne comments, "It was a lot easier than going through the channels, red tape, and negative responses." Wayne's supervisor arranged for an order to be scheduled on the prototype and the results were encouraging, although the set-up time was excessive.

Wayne negotiated with Production Control to run several orders on the electrotrude tooling, thereby making the existence of the tooling public knowledge. Product engineers expressed concern about whether the result-ing wire would pass tests, and closely monitored the production. Many were skeptical of the design because, according to Wayne, "no one really under-stood the concept," except for an engineer who assisted him by selecting the angles of the tooling and preparing several drawings.

In order for the tooling to become officially sanctioned, Wayne had to "get documentation together" in order to justify the design and se-cure more resources to build additional sets of tooling. He accomplished this by "strokin' and talkin'" with people in his own and other departments. Most people cooperated out of friendship or belief that Wayne would re-pay favors.

In compiling the documentation, Wayne entered uncharted territory. Traditionally, operators were not informed about the process of seeking for-mal approval for innovations, and Wayne was unaware of what documents were required, as well as the channels through which they would pass. He also was forced to determine the sort of information required for approval, including the necessary data, determining how to collect them in a manu-facturing setting, and how they are evaluated by decision makers. Finally, he asked engineers for advice on the best way to present his information. In effect, Wayne was not simply documenting an innovation, but also creating procedures to make approval of complex projects accessible to operators.

Wayne proceeded by using a network of friends and acquaintances developed over many years. An engineer, for example, retrieved paperwork from many orders and determined that Wayne's tooling produced less scrap. Even more important, nearly half of the electrotrude-produced lengths of wire were over 5,000 feet; only one-quarter of the lengths produced on traditional tooling were as long.

Wayne's manager assisted by supporting machine scheduling that allowed comparisons demonstrating the efficacy of electrotrude tooling. Engineers assisted in preparing drawings on a computer and in completing several sections of the documentation, such as machining specifications for the tooling. Production Control scheduled orders specifying electrotrude tooling. Wayne's supervisor allowed him to compile the documentation in exchange for helping other operators with their projects.

Despite the successes of the innovation, Wayne comments, "I've had to work to keep it alive. Things die if you don't fan it." Although several sizes of tooling have been fabricated and some orders now specify electrotrude tooling, the latter are directed to Wayne and a few other operators. Wayne says his next task is to secure the cooperation of other operators by educating them about the tooling, and he is already speaking about it at departmental meetings attended by engineers and management.

Wayne continues his research efforts and presently maintains two binders of reference materials for the project. The first includes a summary of how the tooling functions, reviews recommended tooling sizes for different conductor sizes, presents sketches of dies and nipples, and provides a table comparing the yields from electrotrude and tubing set-ups on selected products. The other consists of cost center reports and other records of results he and other operators have achieved.

Wayne remarks, "Electrotrude (tooling) is still my baby," and expects it will continue to be so until more operators can be persuaded to use it. Although coercion could be used, Wayne believes operator consent is essential.

Clearly, electrotrude tooling represents an atypical case, due to both the implications of altering the manufacturing process and the effort and persistence Wayne demonstrated in nurturing it. Yet this project differs only in degree from others, and it provides at least a glimpse of the impact of this sort of participation upon operator tasks and roles. How Wayne "built a case" for his project is the subject of our next discussion.

To begin, Wayne became a more sophisticated generator of information as he learned about the data required to justify allocating resources to the project, as well as how to establish controlled conditions under which to collect data. Wayne commented that it was not enough to demonstrate the efficacy of the tooling; he needed also to understand the costs of developing it and to anticipate the new problems it would undoubtedly create.

As the project coalesced, Wayne compiled documentation to formalize his idea and communicate it to others. This necessitated preparing acceptable drawings, deciding how best to present his ideas, and discussing the ideas in the unambiguous language of engineers. It also exposed Wayne to criticism from others, thereby altering conventional production-floor norms of social interaction.

Perhaps as important as Wayne's technological innovation are his organizational ones: demonstrating to operators, managers, and engineers alike that production-worker innovations can have significant impacts on manufacturing; and effecting procedures to standardize and expedite operator participation. The electrotrude tooling project thus constitutes a transition between the sometimes clandestine operator participation of the "old days"—the domain of tricks and tinkering—and the formalized participation of the present and future.

Building the case for electrotrude tooling also required brief but critical presentations in formal meetings, a trend expected to continue as management and engineers seek a mechanism by which to systematically assess competing claims for resources. Discussion of operator projects is increasingly conducted in formal settings with the various people affected by any innovation presented.

Building the case has also fostered a broader understanding of the production floor and plant organization. Operators, supervisors, and engineers speak of understanding "the big picture," an ambiguous concept that seems to include understanding the functions and agendas of various departments that were previously opaque to operators, as well as envisioning their own department within the overall functioning of the plant.

Wayne was confronted with competing demands for resources from other departments. Previously, he assumed that what was of immediate benefit to his department was obviously desirable, and any objections raised by others were necessarily misguided. Sponsoring this project allowed him to see that other departments had legitimate concerns about his department's actions as well as priorities of their own. Understanding the big picture, too, included learning about the characteristic processes of different areas. For example, Wayne "walked the product" through the production floor to determine if his tooling might have unanticipated consequences elsewhere.

Operators, managers, and engineers concurred in the increasing importance of big-picture knowledge, although its mastery is presently believed to be correlated with an operator's tenure in the plant. However, as opportunities to explore the plant have arisen, it is apparent that some senior operators have little overall understanding of it, while some curious novices rapidly amass big-picture knowledge.

Finally, building the case placed Wayne in the role of advocate. He is adamant that regardless of the inherent efficacy of the tooling, the project requires his constant attention. Rather than be a passive recipient of instructions, the operator as case builder becomes a champion of ideas that he both defends and reevaluates. Likewise, his role as advocate is tempered by the knowledge that if the innovation is successful it will no longer be his, but just another production-floor technology.

REAL WORK

In this chapter we have seen that management's responses to changing market conditions affected the production floor in two ways: It intensified the information-processing tasks of operators and it involved them more deeply in projects intended to improve the workplace. Some of the changes in the operators' tasks can be viewed as mere extensions of existing duties; the increased emphasis on inspections and verification are exemplary. But others represent important discontinuities in what is expected of the operator. Preparing written documentation and participating in public, "on-the-record" meetings transform the communication competencies expected of operators. Developing comprehensive, formalized procedures is not only a new expectation, but it challenges a tacit production-floor tradition of permitting operators to find personally comfortable styles of working. Data collection, experimentation, and hypothesis testing have long been the province of the engineer, and their introduction to the production floor is a radical departure from "getting product out the door." Decision making, negotiating, bargaining, and argumentation, too, have increased dramatically, and while they have their roots in the traditional production-floor culture, they are now defined and expected by management.

Calhoun's new regime constitutes a discontinuity in operator duties, but it does not represent a revolution in the overall allocation of power. Operators, for example, might provide "input" on a new extruder machine control panel, but the decision to purchase it remains with management.

Likewise, Packing operators can complain about the willingness of salesmen to provide customers with new products instead of selling them existing ones, but this decision, too, remains with management.

The previous three chapters have taken us from examining how operators transform raw materials into products, to how they have begun to transform the workplace itself. Although this latter sort of work has only begun (and may be abruptly halted at management's discretion), it has already profoundly altered the tasks operators are expected to perform. These new tasks and the operator's new role are changing the work of producing wire and cable.

Our exploration has also led us away from operators as isolated vessels holding collections of competencies into the workplace as an arena for learning. Operators and supervisors must learn certain knowledge and skills in order to work effectively, and the workplace structures the learning that occurs in it quite independently of formal training. This learning is not isolated to individuals, for all belong to the production-floor community of practice.

7 Learning in Communities of Practice

The first few weeks, you're scared as shit. That machine is running you, you're sure not running it. Some guys will help you and others just say, "No one showed me anything. Figure it out yourself." But now I can run good product without even thinking. I mean I'm here, but I'm really thinking about my hobbies or a fishing trip.

—A senior Extruding operator

New operators arrive on the production floor with little or no experience in making wire and cable, and some have never held a manufacturing job. How these newcomers enter the production floor and its community of practice is the subject of this chapter.

We begin with the decision to hire an applicant, which is but one event in a larger selection process. Potential employees are selected from a pool of applicants on the basis of written tests and repeated interviews. A decision to hire reflects the understandings of supervisors and managers about the characteristics of "good" workers, as well as how those characteristics can be identified in people.

Once hired, new employees undergo training to prepare them to run their machines. Here they encounter trainers who have their own ideas about pedagogy. During this time they learn the basics of running their machines and they assimilate broader lessons about life on the production floor.

Soon the new operators are running machines, while their involvement in the production-floor community of practice develops. They also attend meetings, search for information, ask for assistance, and receive feedback on their performances. Although their attention is on the exigencies of running their machines, they learn about the roles of operators and supervisors, and lessons about a larger, more complex social system. How to protect themselves and provide accounts for their actions are crucial lessons quickly learned. They also become enculturated into a production-floor worldview that helps them interpret the behavior of others, as well as construct appropriate performances for other operators, engineers, and management.

SELECTION AND HIRING

Individuals take their first step toward employment when they complete the standard application in Techno Industries' employment office. Applicants receiving favorable assessments are called back to complete a comprehensive test that assesses reading, basic arithmetic, and communications skills. They also complete a form that prompts them to write brief paragraphs about several personal and work experiences.

Favorable evaluations on these two assessment tools lead to an interview, the goal of which is to determine the applicant's ability and willingness to learn new skills. Applicants are then interviewed at the individual facilities that hire them. At Calhoun, this entails interviews with the production manager, a departmental manager, and several supervisors. Operators, too, often participate in these interviews.

Because the arithmetic, reading, and writing abilities of applicants have been assessed, interviewers look instead for other indications that the person can become a competent worker. This task was previously simpler because workers were hired for specific job openings where they often remained for years. Later, as part of the plant reorganization, operators were hired based on their potential to assume progressively more responsible positions.

The supervisors, who conduct most of the interviews, develop informal profiles of the "good worker" that guide their assessments. The attributes sought may be categorized as technical competence, attitudes toward work, social skills, and work habits. Few if any operators arrive with the technical skills needed to make wire and cable, but some supervisors believe that mechanical ability is desirable. Supervisors agree that comfort with and agility around machinery is necessary, as are broad problem-solving skills. All cite a positive, enthusiastic attitude to work as critical, as well as being willing and able to work with other people. Supervisors mention the importance of work habits such as attendance, reliability, self-management, and flexibility.

Striking in the supervisors' profiles of the good operator is the relative unimportance of technical skills and the premium placed on positive attitude, working well with others, and diligent work habits. This emphasis is reflected, too, in their beliefs about what distinguishes average from excellent operators. Five of seven supervisors mentioned motivation and commitment to work as critical, and the other two cited a willingness to initiate actions that improve the workplace; improved technical skills were never mentioned.

Operators also have ideas about the attributes of good workers. A Packing operator commented, "Everyone here is a sweetheart," noting that he was readily accepted by his coworkers despite his eccentric appearance. "They hire based on personality, but in a good way. They get nice people. And if you can't fit in, you're gone. You'll never make it." Another remarked, "They're lenient here. If you mess up an order you won't be fired, but if you're absent a lot or tardy, you will be. It's like school: There are rules and you have to be here."

Other operators noted that the nature of the work requires that they work with others. One remarked, "Being a troubleshooter is stressful, and to do it you have to be nice to everyone. You have to deal with everyone in the plant, including people on the other side [in administration]. Personality is important. You also need common sense and the ability to learn new things all the time. And it helps to feel good when you solve a problem." A senior extruder operator expressed a widespread sentiment when he noted, "You have to be able to work with others. There's no way you can survive out there by yourself."

Despite the similarity of operator and supervisor profiles of the good worker, the operators mentioned additional attributes. Attention to detail was widely cited, including carefully reviewing paperwork, closely monitoring the product, and working diligently on difficult products. Mechanical ability was often mentioned, but its definition varied. For some operators it is a familiarity with tools and machines, while for others it refers to feeling comfortable around machinery. Many operators explained that mechanical ability means a level of physical coordination or agility that prevents injuries. For others, it is the ability to analyze problems. The attribute of common sense, too, was widely mentioned in interviews. Learning how to demonstrate it is critical, and an operator who fails to do so develops a poor reputation among his or her colleagues.

Because the operator's potential to perform in future positions is salient, interviewers make important predictions based on very limited information. These assessments are especially important since supervisors and managers concur that the company can do little to modify fundamental attitudes and social skills. One supervisor noted, "You have people for eight hours a day. They have their whole life outside. Many have family problems, or God knows what, and you just can't change that. This is a business, not the Navy, and there's a limit to what you can do."

Interviewers develop strategies to test for desired attributes. Some try to engage the applicant in stories about their previous employment. "If there's nothing they felt enthusiastic about or proud of, if it's all just sort of flat and dreary, I won't hire them," one said. Others look for indicators of drive and ambition: "I want someone who wants to be a self-manager and grow into new jobs. I really like it if they want to own their own business someday, whatever it is." Previous employment is considered indicative of the potential to succeed on the production floor. Applicants who have worked in manufacturing environments or who otherwise have worked with machinery are generally deemed to possess the requisite aptitude. Even hobbies are considered revealing, and many interviewers ask about them: "I ask about their hobbies. If they work on cars, or they have a workbench in their garage, I figure they'll make it."

Under the mandate for increased operator participation, an operator typically interviews each applicant with personal ideas about testing for requisite attributes. One remarked, "I try to position the person, you know, fence them in so they're near a machine. If they're uncomfortable and try to get away, I'd worry. I look for the guy who looks like he wants to get his hands on that machine!" His coworker concurred and added, "If I had a choice between hiring a farm boy from Willits [a rural northern California town] with no history of being a wage earner, and an urban kid who has a work history, I'd unquestionably hire the farm boy. Living on a farm you learn how to get things to work without asking for help."

Of course, there are disagreements about both attributes and tests. One operator claimed, "I would never hire a kid who had worked at McDonald's. They do learn that they have to show up to be paid, but after ten minutes of instruction they've mastered the job and they'll never make more than minimum wage. They don't learn initiative, creativity, all the things they need in a job that pays more." But another volunteered, "I look for someone who's worked in fast-food places since they know how to work hard and are disciplined."

Despite these differences, Calhoun's standard written testing generally assures that new operators have minimal basic skills in reading, writing, and arithmetic, and the interviewing process generally selects people with some variant of mechanical ability. More recently, operators who demonstrate enthusiasm, a willingness to work and improve the workplace, and an ability to get along with coworkers have been selected.

TRAINING

After being hired, applicants complete an orientation at corporate headquarters, where they listen to speakers, participate in several exercises, and watch a videotape, all intended to convey information about the corporation. The corporate values of "freedom, structure, risk, and decision making" are presented, and participants are told that the corporation values strong individuals who can work in a group context; the metaphor of an ensemble of musicians conveys the image of dedicated people who direct their individual talents toward collective goals.

The next day, the newly hired operator begins training on the production floor. Formal training generally includes "classroom" instruction, coaching in how to perform basic tasks, and opportunities to ask questions. Packing Department is the entry portal for most new operators, and its training program is the most formalized. The newcomer is assigned to one trainer for a month and receives a thick binder of materials to memorize. Trainers are in turn guided by checklists of the information trainees are expected to assimilate each week.

Operators are also trained by other departments. Extruding operators typically undergo a one-week training class that describes the flow of work, product documentation, numbering systems, parts of an extruder, elementary principles of the process, and characteristics of extruder tooling. Following this classroom training, operators usually work alongside an experienced colleague for a week or two, after which they are assigned a machine, with a nearby colleague to assist.

The content of training naturally varies among areas, and supervisors differ in the credence they give classroom instruction, pencil-and-paper examinations, the duration of training, and the preparation of training materials. In general, training is implemented erratically, and many operators commented that they were exceptions to the rule of their department or area.

Not surprisingly, Calhoun's supervisors and operators alike believe that the purpose of training is to transfer requisite skills and knowledge to the novice. Yet trainers are modest in their claims about the contribution training makes toward an operator's ultimate success. Realistically, it only lays the foundation for the trainee to begin to run machines while simultaneously drawing on the assistance of more senior operators.

The core task of training is conceptualized as "learning the basics," although doing so is ambiguous, for three reasons. First, the conceptualization of algorithmic, procedural knowledge that is conveyed in the classroom and its relationship to practice varies among departments and trainers. In some areas, classroom pedagogy is deemed appropriate for conveying abstract principles about a process, information about the flow of work through the area, or numbering systems for products. Procedural knowledge about how to actually perform basic tasks is believed to follow from running the machines under a trainer's watchful eye. In other areas, the basics consist of algorithms for performing some common tasks which must be committed to memory prior to engaging a machine. Thus, the relationship of plans to action is conceptualized diversely and shapes the conduct of training.

Second, the basics are necessarily presented by operators who possess their own styles, and differentiating between that which is standard and personal idiosyncrasies can be difficult. A Marking area operator's conclusion was typical: "I always felt I had to check out whether what my trainer told me was just his way of doing it." Not only can styles differ, but trainers are often unaware that some of their practices are contraindicated. "Lots of what the older operators think is right is incorrect," another remarked. "I actually know more about the right way than some of them."

A recurring issue in many departments is whether training should present a single, basic style from which new operators may build, or alternative ways of performing identical tasks. Most departments strive toward the former, but a lack of consensus militates against it. Because alternative ways of performing tasks are seldom systematically compared, each may be deemed equally efficacious, thereby protecting the reputations of "master" operators. The novice, of course, is unclear about the differences between the universal and idiosyncratic aspects of running machines, as well as the reputations and abilities of different operators, and accordingly must sort them out.

Third, training is more than an instrumental activity: It is the setting in which operators first encounter deeper issues regarding power, learning, and training in the workplace. The changes in company policies about training over time demarcate different cohorts of operators, and newcomers today hear tales about their seniors who learned to operate machines with minimal assistance. While some of these veterans are exemplary trainers, others train only grudgingly. Arthur, a veteran of over two decades, explained: "I'll tell them what to do a couple of times, but you can't teach people much. I leave 'em alone. Let 'em use their heads. That's the way I learned it. I train them like I was trained [laughs]: Nobody told me anything."

Arthur was explicit in his refusal to serve as a trainer, and he has acquired a poor reputation among supervisors and his peers. Other operators who share his feelings are subtler. Eddie, a veteran Marking area operator, recounted that operators can be trained to read paperwork, set up their machines, and solve very routine problems, but not to handle extraordinary problems. He concluded, "They learn by watching the master operators work." Nevertheless, a junior operator laughed as he recalled his own experience with Eddie:

I'd always had trouble with that product, so I asked Eddie if he'd show me how to run it. I'd heard he was the best. So he said "OK," and I stayed after my shift till he started. Things would go wrong, and he'd send me off to get something. But when I'd get back, he'd have done something to fix it, and he wouldn't tell me what. Or he'd do it and just turn so I couldn't quite see. He didn't want me to see. I never asked him for anything again, 'cause lots of other guys are more helpful.

New operators thus learn about making wire and cable during their formal training and as they ask for help from colleagues, but they also learn about the history of the plant and how different operators integrate the role of trainer into their jobs. They learn that in the eyes of many, they are privileged learners who are provided, at no cost to themselves, the hard-won expertise of their elders. For their part, junior operators often prefer to be trained by operators with three to five years of experience rather than by senior masters. This is partially due to similarities in age and the recency of their own training, but some operators (and engineers) remarked that many newer operators become better informed about the technical exigencies of their jobs.

Trainers' attitudes also shape their views of cross-training. As part of the new organizational regime, operators are assigned for periods of three to sixth months to different areas or departments. The twin goals of cross-training are to increase flexibility in scheduling workers during weekends and vacations, and to increase the operators' overall knowledge of the plant.

Many operators see cross-training as a way to increase their job security, reduce the tedium of remaining in one area, and ensure their share of overtime. New operators are hired understanding that they will be cross-trained. One remarked, "I like it. I want to be cross-trained anywhere, because it just makes me more valuable to the company. Lots of the older guys hate it and don't want to do it."

Although not all senior operators dislike cross-training, and many agreed that it allowed them to better understand the plant, opposition to cross-training is concentrated among them. According to one veteran extruder operator, "They [supervisors] move people around a lot, and it can be hard to get back to your area. They don't want people to be masters." A senior operator commented that he had been moved to Shielding area for eighteen months and when he returned to Cabling area, "I had to start all over. I had to start from the basics." He went on to explain that cross-training increased his uncertainty: "When you leave, you don't know what you will be running tomorrow, so you don't feel like putting all you've got into it. I used to plan my next day's work at home, but now I don't because I don't know where I'll be." Ironically, this operator had been assigned to the same machine for the entire preceding year. Still, the sentiment that cross-training is an attack on an operator's mastery of his or her machine is widespread.

As they undergo training, operators are exposed to theories about learning and instruction, especially the relationship between abstract knowledge conveyed in classrooms and the hands-on knowledge gained from operating a machine. There is a robust suspicion of classroom instruction, and tales abound of operators who were first in their class but who failed to master their machines. Other stories involve trainees who stumbled in the classroom but who thrived once they were able to get their hands on a machine. Dwight's story is exemplary: "I've been here a year and barely know the basics. When I took the extrusion class I almost failed it. There were five of us, and I was last. But once we got on the machines, I learned faster than anyone. I guess I'm a hands-on kinda learner."

Robert, a senior Cabling area operator, recounted that some college-educated trainees find it difficult to run the relatively simple machines of the area. "I remember one guy who had no mechanical ability. I showed him over and over how to start it up. I mean, you push down two buttons and turn one pot[entiometer]. But he never caught on and was always asking me to show him again. Lots of college-educated people want to begin with the manual, which they hope will have all the information they need." He tells them that there are no "complete textbooks," but they still write everything down in a notebook. Robert then tells them that they cannot accumulate the knowledge to address all eventualities: "You might be the one to have happen to you something that no one has seen before. You need to know the machine's capabilities and have a theory of operation. You need a gut feel for the machines and a willingness to pick the brains of the other operators."

These two examples illustrate several facets of popular models of learning and training. Operators learn to think of their own learning in terms of a style. Some are "theoretical learners," yet Dwight exemplifies the classic "hands-on learner" who succeeds in spite of his classroom failure.

Conceptualizations of training also vary, affecting the experience of trainees. Robert exemplifies the thoughtful operator who theorizes about learning styles and training and who adjusts his training accordingly. He is not alone in his theorizing, and other trainers attempt to rectify what they see as mistakes in their own training. A junior Packing operator recalled, "It's up to the trainer to organize it right. I spent my first two days doing nothing but sitting behind the spooler with my hands on the wire. I learned nothing about paperwork, really. When I have a chance to train, I have the trainees fill in all the paperwork from day one, with me sitting there telling them how to do it."

Trainers vary in their willingness to share information with newcomers, some reasoning that to do so is to relinquish a hard-earned resource, others that sharing knowledge is an investment in a network of helpers. One commented, "You know, it helps your reputation to be known as a good trainer. You get plum assignments when they come up, and people you trained owe you. You can go to them later for help or favors."

Trainers differ, too, in the abilities that they feel underlie success on the production floor, and this affects how they deliver training. Some operators rely extensively on memory augmented by years of experience; formal training here makes a comparatively small contribution to becoming skilled. Others believe that the best operators are careful analysts of problems, so they spend considerable time explaining their troubleshooting strategies to trainees.

Ideas about learning styles and appropriate training reflect assumptions that both trainers and trainees make about themselves and the production floor. The training therefore clearly reflects the accommodations individual operators have made to the new regime. In this sense, training is as much a political statement as an activity performed to impart technical skills. Theories of learning styles also define people as particular types (e.g., "theoretical" or "mechanical"), which may not be so adaptive under conditions of technological change.

Practice and Feedback

Gradually, the new operators assume more responsibility on the production floor. At first, they are assigned to run machines while a trainer observes their progress. Within a week, the trainer's role shifts to that of an assistant to be called upon when problems arise. Lessons large and small are learned as the operator asks for help, engages new colleagues in conversation, and listens to them discuss life on the production floor.

Operators soon learn about the often complex relationships between production work and technology. Central here is the belief that each machine is unique. When combined with the vast number of distinct products, seemingly infinite numbers of permutations arise. In the extreme, every order is the result of a contingent process controlled only by the operator's vigilance, experience, and memory. In Extruding, for example, operators discuss the several-hundred distinct insulating compounds, some of which differ from batch to batch. Tales are told of operators able to detect such variations by smelling or chewing on a single pellet of material. Veteran Shielding area operators concurred that the dozens of seemingly identical machines have been rebuilt so many times that each has its own character.

Regardless of variety in machines or raw materials, the operator must learn to "stay in the [product] window" while running an order. This metaphorical window is formed by a set of variables such as weights, diameters, and lays. Each product must fall within an acceptable range for each variable. Acceptable lots of the same product are thus categorically identical (i.e., good or bad), but in reality they differ slightly in characteristics.

The concept of "staying in the window" has important implications for learning. First, operators may run their machines somewhat differently and still produce good wire. In this way, new operators learn that different run conditions produce acceptable products, thereby reinforcing both the operators' right to comfort and their claims to proficiency. The validity of these claims is, of course, a function of the size of the product window: If engineers suddenly narrow or otherwise change it, some previously good lots will become unacceptable. When this occurs, an operator's ability may be questioned.

Second, operators may develop preferences for "running in the center of the window," or for "chasing the window." For example, some extruding machine operators immediately "pull out" of an order and install new tooling if they are nearing the "edge of the window." Others, in the interests of efficiency, delay and remain longer with a dubious set-up. To do so is to "chase the window," and the resulting product may be only marginally "in spec." While the first approach is formally sanctioned, produces a more standard product, and arguably requires less downtime, it also makes for prosaic performances by the operator. The second approach often makes for good theater as the operator struggles to keep the product "in the window" despite all odds, even though those odds were self-imposed. Many junior operators are impressed by these performances and aspire to such virtuosity instead of the more mundane path of changing tooling.

Despite their best efforts, operators sometimes fail to produce acceptable products, and the new operator soon learns about "dinging." To "ding" another area usually means to detect a fault produced by it; alternatively, a ding may refer to the variance per se. Operators demonstrate competence by detecting the faults of others while minimizing their own. Dinging provides feedback about quality throughout the plant, but it can be contentious since when faults cross organizational boundaries potential adversaries become involved. Dinging is thus not only a means of error detection, but simultaneously a threat to reputations and careers.

Dinging involves considerable interpretation by supervisors, as well as operators whose opinions and reputations may be at risk. It must be determined if the evidence indicates a fault and, if so, which machines or operators are to blame. Faults are also evaluated against a sometimes shifting standard of acceptability. For example, the same product made for two customers may be evaluated differently, and the product's use can affect judgment.

A ding is thus the outcome of an often lengthy and contentious interpretive endeavor, and veteran operators educate their often inexperienced supervisors about its nuances. Specifically, they remind their supervisors that others have incentives to make accusations, and that there are costs if they succeed. Senior operators claim it is important to allow operators to explain themselves or to rebut accusations.

Despite its ubiquity, dinging provides a limited basis for learning. Data collected about run conditions may be less than accurate, and the operator may be unable to associate specific run conditions with the outcomes due to the passage of time. Precise, immediate feedback that connects run conditions to outcomes on a reel-by-reel basis is largely absent, and in lieu of it, individual operators may develop their own data bases concerning particular products or processes. Many cultivate friendships among potential helpers such as engineers, technicians, and operators in adjacent areas.

The relevance of the product window and dinging cannot be underestimated. They constrain how operators learn about the results of their actions, while they also mold the performances that are valued as evidence of competence on the production floor. Most important, they reveal how formal training provides only limited lessons to the new operator: The workplace independently imparts equally important lessons through the daily experience of work.

LARGER LESSONS

As newcomers become more familiar with running machines, they learn larger lessons about the production floor. These are conveyed in stories and conversations, and they are inferred by watching the interactions of coworkers. They take the operator further away from his or her concerns about processing an order, and they are central to the operator's participation in the community of practice.[1]

Operators soon learn that they possess resources that are valued by supervisors and engineers, which affect their relationships with them. The historic instability of the production process, coupled with management's desire to improve it and the organizational norms of individuals, provides the basis for operator power. Operators routinely provide engineers with information about particular orders or pet projects, and engineers readily concede that operators are their "eyes and ears" on the production floor. This informal feedback is especially prized by engineers who are responsible for a multitude of products.

Engineers, too, recognize the need for operator cooperation. One noted that he was training a senior Marking area operator to run a new machine so other operators would be able to use it, and so the senior operator could not oppose it. More generally, a senior engineer remarked, "If the operators don't like a new piece of technology they won't use it, and the idea that it won't work circulates. Getting 'buy-in' matters."

The relationship between operators and supervisors is especially complex, and while the latter have clear authority over their departments, they exercise this power carefully to secure the operators' cooperation. Supervisors are expected to have some college education and ideally a college degree. This restricts promotion from within, and many supervisors now lack the technical expertise of their predecessors. As a result, operators communicate directly with the engineers and technicians who can provide needed technical expertise.

Because the supervisor's position is often a stepping-stone for college graduates destined to work elsewhere in Techno Industries, most remain in the position for only a few years. Operators discuss their need to train their supervisors, and they do so—often grudgingly—as an investment in their own careers. A well-trained supervisor can capture resources for an operator and support the latter's pet projects. However, many operators feel that supervisors move on just when they are in a position to repay this debt.

As their tenure on the production floor lengthens, operators also learn how to request assistance, thereby entering a world of mutual obligations. Operators differ in their reputations for offering and receiving assistance, and an important task for the rookie operator is to nurture a network of helpers. In some areas, rookies are subjected to practical jokes, such as instructions to retrieve nonexistent tools like the legendary "left-handed wire stretcher." Operators accept this hazing since they rely on some of the culprits for help. Furthermore, unless the perpetrators are fired, the rookie fears creating enemies and developing a reputation as someone who "can't take it."

Asking for help must be carefully managed. A new operator reflected, "You have to act just right. If you're arrogant or a 'know it all,' they won't help. They'll just wait for you to blow it. But if you're too quiet and nice, they'll eat you up playing tricks." Requests for assistance may even be met with deliberate misinformation, resulting in scrap. Operators in each area pointed out others who provided either unreliable information or none at all. A senior extruder operator remarked, "There are some older guys out there who'll watch you fuck up all day. They'll know exactly what's wrong and how to fix it, but they'll never say anything. Other guys—Wayne, Loren—they'll always come over if you're having problems."

Help is therefore not always forthcoming, and even when it is, the operator must assess the veracity of the advice. The operator is often faced with eliciting assistance, assessing contradictory advice, and taking a course of action, for ultimately she is responsible for the order. But she must manage this without offending those whose advice she ignores, since she will likely need their help again. Operators manage this task with varying degrees of effort and success: Some can immediately obtain accurate information from many operators, while others are able to mobilize only one or two others who may possess inadequate information.

Broader lessons concern the admonition to "protect yourself." Most obviously, operators attempt to minimize importing variances from other areas and to avoid exporting variances that could lead to dinging. Routines for inspecting inputs and outputs are the primary means for this buffering, and they are a formal part of the operator's job.

Less formally, operators learn to account for their actions in the event that they are later challenged by supervisors. For example, a Marking area operator said that if his replacement had not arrived by the end of his shift, he would shut down all his machines: "Otherwise I may be blamed for any problems and the operator may not even show up." Operators in all areas similarly protected themselves.

Another manifestation of accountability occurs when operators seek approvals from supervisors. An extruder operator reported that, although he efficiently tries to schedule cleanouts of his machine, "sometimes this can seem to shift tasks to the next shift, so when I 'jump schedule' I always get the supervisor's approval to cover myself." A well-regarded rookie spooler said that when he encountered problems, "I consult with my lead, never another operator, because there are too many things operators do differently. By going to the lead I protect myself and also learn the correct way to handle the problem."

Even supervisors' attempts to ensure accountability may become contentious. A Cabling area operator remarked that he and his colleagues were required to verify that they had read the manual for one machine by signing a list. When asked what signing meant, the operator responded, "It means if you screw up on something mentioned in it, you're in trouble!" He refused to sign, since while he had read the manual he did not feel qualified to run the machine. In fact, he hoped his refusal would provoke better training.

The quest for accountability is reflected in the preference for written verification. Many operators refuse to accept verbal approvals: Written approval both protects the operator and is evidence of the supervisor's confidence in a decision. Most senior operators told tales of supervisors forgetting what they had approved, or even reneging on their word. Thus, most await approval for any but the most trivial changes in handling a product. Obtaining such approvals often involves tactful conversations with supervisors who may be offended by an operator's refusal to accept a verbal approval.

Finally, operators learn to "be efficient." Some practices are clearly efficient, such as retrieving sufficient supplies for the duration of a shift and minimizing trips to obtain new tooling. Ideally, efficient operators will assist nearby colleagues or prepare material for the next order when their machines are running satisfactorily, then complete paperwork before letting the machines sit idle.

Being efficient is complex, however, and measuring efficiency and comparing ways to be efficient are rarely undertaken. Minimizing cleanouts of the extruder barrel is a classic efficiency strategy, and Elmore's strategy is representative. He was assigned three orders using the same diameter conductor, but with different-colored insulation: 200,000 feet of white, 8,000 feet of black, and 200,000 feet of yellow. One cleanout is required during each shift, and Elmore prefers that it be made at a "natural break." The cleanout was due after the first 200,000-foot order, but Elmore claimed that 8,000 feet more doesn't matter. After completing the first order and bleeding the white compound from the extruder barrel, he added black pellets to the hopper and ran the second order. Then he shut it down and performed the cleanout. Finally, he loaded the third order and filled the cleaned machine with fresh compound and yellow coloring.

Elmore could have cleaned the machine after the first order, but he knew a cleanout was also necessary before switching from a dark to a light-color compound. He assumed the compound would not degrade while he ran another 8,000 feet of wire, a safe bet for an experienced operator. Elmore commented, "The operator can do this, but if you're wrong you gotta be prepared to pull out [and perform the cleanout] fast."

Several features of the quest for efficiency stand out. The cyclical nature of many conditions is striking. Operators avoid short reels of conductor and prefer long ones that minimize machine downtime, but of course all reels are eventually used. And while better and worse sequences of orders undoubtedly exist, cleanouts are eventually performed.

Less clear are the effects of efficiency strategies on the overall pattern of production. The eight-hour shift is the frame of reference for most operators, and their assessment of efficiency reflects this perspective. The extruder operator may seek to minimize *his* downtime, but may actually increase the total number of cleanouts and lower productivity, all in the name of efficiency. Furthermore, delaying cleanouts on some products may result in slightly degraded compound such that the wire later fails a test. Operators are typically unaware of these outcomes and thus continue the practices that produce them.

The larger lessons we have discussed are seldom the object of formal instruction, but they are learned nonetheless. Mastering them identifies the operator as a savvy individual, one who knows the actual workings of the production floor and who can navigate its local politics. And their mastery further marks the operator as a member of the community of practice.

ORGANIZATIONAL WORLDVIEW

We have traced how operators who first confront getting an order "up and running" learn progressively broader lessons about the production floor. These lessons are learned piecemeal and sometimes inconsistently, but they reflect a deeper worldview (Kearney 1984) consisting of assumptions about the individual, society, environment, and causality. These allow operators to interpret the actions of others and to produce appropriate performances themselves. Gradually, operators are enculturated into this organizational worldview.

The idea of an organizational worldview must, however, be approached carefully.[2] Operators live only part of their daily lives on the production floor, and the latter is limited in its capacity to shape thoughts and actions. To the extent that we can identify a production-floor worldview it will not be unique but will reflect distinctions drawn from a wider society. Yet, while no claim is made that the production floor constitutes a world unto itself, it is somewhat distinct from comparable workplaces.

As we have seen throughout our discussions, the community of practice is marked by an individualism in which operators have the right to be left alone and work comfortably. Many engineers, too, hold the view that operators do best if left to their own devices; indeed, the plant has a history of asking operators to "do your best" under trying conditions.

Individuals are expected to direct their efforts to the benefit of the entire plant, not to self-aggrandizement. The remarks of an Extruding area supervisor during a private meeting with one operator are illustrative. The operator had been working diligently but had failed to provide adequate guidance to several workers assigned to his area. The supervisor explained, "You gotta take the time to plan. I want you to organize it the way you want it for everyone's benefit." This mandate to take individual responsibility to act for everyone's benefit is widespread, and a hallmark of the well-socialized operator.

Individualism is inculcated during training and reinforced daily on the production floor. Although trainers view the transmission of technical skills and knowledge as their paramount goal, meeting the needs of individual trainees is explicitly acknowledged. A Cabling area operator, for example, said, "I've done training, and I always try to show them the easy way to do it, but I never insist that they do it my way. I'd never tell them how they have to do it." A senior extruding operator commented, "Every operator I train, I train to use a system. They don't have to do it my way, but they have to develop some sort of system to make the work easier, to minimize downtime and wasted materials."

Trainees are also given many chances to find a trainer who will meet their idiosyncratic needs. An operator who had organized training for Packing reported: "We don't really reject too many people: We work with those people like Alfred who take more time. There are lots of operators to help out." And an extruder operator told of his own first months on the job: "I messed up really bad a few times, specially when I was starting out, but I've never been given hell for it. They always knew I was trying as hard as I could."

The sentiments that trainers should offer but not impose their expertise, and that operators differ in their strengths and weaknesses are explicitly supported by supervisors. Homer, the Extruding area supervisor we met before, assessed training in his area as relatively unstructured but focused on meeting operator needs: "There's nothing so that any Joe Blow could come in off the street and be trained. But from day one I talk with the trainee to find out what he needs as an individual." Although Homer knows that "they are expected to do certain things—that is not negotiable," the supervisor's larger challenge is "building up people's confidence and importance." He continued, "Everyone is above average. It's just up to me to find where. The most important thing is that they have a sense of confidence in themselves." Another supervisor noted, "I owe all my employees so they can grow either into other jobs here, or as human beings who can take some of this outside [of Calhoun]."

Respect for the individual is thus a basic production-floor value. Supervisors believe that mastering the technical tasks is the easiest challenge to meet: Training and time on the job will suffice. More difficult is finding ways to gradually incorporate uniquely talented operators so they can use those talents for the benefit of everyone on the production floor. Operators who serve as trainers replicate this individualism, although their motives may be quite different. And trainees who were able to recall their own early experiences confirmed their colleagues' willingness to demonstrate and explain, but not to impose specific ways of running orders.

If enlightened individualism is virtuous, those individuals must fit into larger work groups, and on the production floor the metaphor of family is ubiquitous. Supervisors and operators alike concurred about the plant's reputation as a family-like place that is both supportive and demanding. The plant has the reputation of firing few workers for their mistakes, and most who are terminated have histories of chronic absenteeism, conflict with coworkers, and poor attitude. However, communication can be quite open and frank. One supervisor commented, "I've been burned a few times in meetings, and now I really watch what I say. You have to have a thick skin."

Calhoun may be family-like, but operators learn to make other distinctions among people. They hear stories about the reputations of different areas, and they observe the attributes of operators assigned to them. Theorizing about the characteristics of an area's machines and the nature of the work performed there, and especially about gender and ethnicity, is a popular sport.

For example, Extruding is said to require mathematical and mechanical skills, and its operators have long been at the peak of the production-floor hierarchy. "'You ain't shit unless you run an extruder,' that's their attitude," said a spooling machine operator. "It's the land of the white male," said an Extruding area supervisor, commenting on the relative absence of women, African Americans, and Hispanic Americans from the department. In contrast, the Cabling area was considered by many operators to be the simplest and most stable process, but one that required responsible operators due to the costliness of mistakes in assembling a complex cable. The area attracted many Hispanic workers, and relatively few women.

All areas are subject to theorizing, and machine or process attributes, ethnicity, and gender are widely thought to intersect in ways that attract some operators and repel others. The Packing Department is the object of extensive theorizing since the majority of its operators are women, and their concentration there was even greater in the past. The present supervisor spoke nostalgically of that past and wished he could hire even more women since he claimed they are better spoolers. However, the plant is committed to reducing gender disparities among the areas, and in Packing that means more male operators.

Packing is thus a department in which female operators have been valued. Michelle, a female lead operator, speculated that the spooling machine is simple and easy to run and is not as intimidating as are, for example, extruding machines, which require that operators master an elaborate control panel, navigate around high temperatures, and hoist heavy loads. Packing requires no mechanical troubleshooting, but processing orders does require extensive product knowledge and meticulous work habits.

Michelle claimed that "spooling seems too menial, too sedentary" to the plant's males, since the operator must remain at the machine in order to process orders. Packing is also known as the most "social" of the departments. The machines are positioned in two rows with a single wide aisle between them so the operators can easily watch one another. "They won't admit it, but they compete very hard to look good in front of their peers. It's not security-related, but a desire to express themselves in a style that's theirs," Michelle explained. Productivity is part of this competition, but putting up an order in a distinctive style is the basis for pride.

Not all operators or supervisors would, of course, agree entirely with Michelle's assessment of gender in Packing. Many account for the concentration of women by pointing to the department's relative cleanliness making it less factory-like. Others remarked that the prejudices of male operators in other areas are more significant, and they cited rumors of female trainees receiving inadequate instruction from their male trainers.

Regardless of assessment, the topic of gender in the workplace evokes strong responses from many workers. The supervisor who assigned the first man to the Packing Department recalled that he complained, "You've just cut off my balls," and became so ill that he visited a physician. Female operators, too, disagree about the proper places for men and women in the plant. One woman who worked in Marking area identified herself as a "machine person" who will move anywhere to operate machinery; she dismissed spooling as "not real work." Others commented that they would never work in Packing because, as one noted, "They're too cliquish."

We may conclude that new operators soon learn that gender matters in the community of practice, but precisely how and why is the subject of disputation. Despite differences of opinion, gender cannot be ignored and operators soon develop theories about its importance. Comparable speculation about ethnicity also occurs.

Another distinction made by operators is between "short-termers" who have worked in the plant less than about three years and "long-termers" who have been employed at least five, and often as many as twenty, years. For some operators, these terms also signify an operator's plans for employment. For example, one operator who planned to work for several years was called a short-termer, while his friend called himself a long-termer: "I'm planning on being an operator a long time. I like the company and I'm willing to do what they want because they'll support me." Many senior operators noted sardonically that they had been short-termers, but as one remarked, "Marriage, kids, house, boat, you know, and I'm still here."

The effects of longevity contribute to structuring the community of practice. First, operators hired at different times may have been hired for different reasons, with earlier cohorts being hired to fill a specific position and more recent ones hired for their potential to fill presently unknown positions. Earlier hires, for example, were not explicitly hired for their communication skills, while this is now a formal criterion.

Second, operators were trained during different managerial regimes, which affected their initial experiences in the plant. Some employees with over two decades on the job still speak of the difficulty of their first few weeks and months in the plant, and they decline to assist today's newly hired coworkers. Others with similar memories are generous in their assistance.

Third, operators with more time in the plant are necessarily more experienced. They have encountered more idiosyncratic products and many are viewed as walking archives of product and process knowledge, although they may resist sharing that knowledge. They also have very developed and often unconscious styles of running their machines, although in some cases their knowledge has not kept up with current practice. Many junior operators recognize the knowledge of senior operators, but they conclude much of it is outdated, and they place more trust in their own judgment.

For their part, many senior operators scoff at the claims of their juniors to have mastered an area. One senior Extruding area operator laughed and commented, "The older operator is reasonably confident; the younger is certain." Another identified a group of "knot-tiers" who can splice a new order to the tail end of the preceding one, but who are unable to set up the machine.

Beliefs about the physical environment also comprise an important part of the worldview. Machines constitute the most obvious element of the physical environment, and operator attitudes about them are complex. On the one hand, they adapt to the machines without complaint. For example, a marking machine operator commented during a meeting that newly added pulleys restricted the operator's view of the wire speeding past. Learning to see the mark would be especially difficult for new operators who might even catch their fingers in the pulleys. However, the area's master operator, Pablo, argued: "They'll get used to it. It's the job of the operator to adjust to the machine."

Here, machine characteristics set the stage for virtuoso performances by the operator and contribute to defining his or her primary responsibility.

On the other hand, machines can be modified, and tinkering provides tempting opportunities to demonstrate problem-solving abilities. Individual operators are neither exclusively adaptors or modifiers; in fact, Pablo is a notorious tinkerer. But arguments can typically be made on a case-by-case basis that skill is best demonstrated by adapting to inefficient machinery or tinkering with it.

Adaptation and modification are also related to attitudes about involvement in projects to improve the workplace. Operators have historically accepted the conditions under which they process wire and cable with minimal comment: The right and responsibility to set those conditions belong to management. The present regime of participation through projects places the operator in the role of working on those workplace conditions and not merely adapting to them.

Attitudes about the physical environment are even more dramatically displayed during debates about "art" and "science." The artistic view is based on the ubiquity of variances and operator styles: Identical conditions seemingly lead to different outcomes, and some operators jokingly speak of the "black art" of running their machines. Operator intuition, honed by years of experience, is celebrated and formal, written procedures are viewed skeptically. In the extreme, everything is contingent and the operator becomes the ever-vigilant guardian against threats to meeting customer deadlines.

The scientific view rests on the assumption that the production process can in principle be specified in terms of precise measurements, even if those measurements are presently unavailable. The feel of a wire, for instance, now assessed by plucking it, could be measured by a meter, even if to date such meters have proven inadequate. The goal here is better control over the process and a more standardized product.

Like the debate between adaptation and modification, the one between art and science is complex, its features vary by area, and operators often maintain inconsistent positions about it. The Marking area is an important site in which the case for art is argued. During one meeting a technician tried to introduce a gauge that allows the operators to compute the angle at which an ink stripe is applied to the wire. Pablo retorted, "But you know, science isn't everything. Art comes into it, too." The technician responded that the gauge contributes to a more standard product and besides, few operators have Pablo's twenty years of experience. But Pablo countered by informing his coworkers that such a gauge is unsatisfactory because "the angles it gives aren't the ones you use to get a nice-looking product."

Another component of worldview concerns causality or, more explicitly, the construction of common sense. According to supervisors, engineers, and operators, this is the most important operator skill. It is most clearly manifested in the operator's ability to load, set up, and adjust the orders she runs, and to troubleshoot the inevitable problems that arise.

Lapses in common sense occur in two different ways: deviating from or compulsively adhering to established procedures. In the former, operators fail to perform a standard, established set-up, or they prematurely deviate from it. The latter lapse is exhibited when an operator fails to recognize that he/she *should* deviate from procedures and, as several operators said, "try something different."

An example from the Extruding area illustrates the issues involved. Simon took over an order that the previous operator had spent four hours trying to set up. He commented that the operator correctly "went by the book" but should have asked for help or "changed something" after several hours. Simon helped train the operator and judges him "a very good one," but he is "too mechanical, not flexible, not creative."

Simon double-checked the machine set-up and performed his troubleshooting routine. After an hour, he commented, "Common sense says, 'Do something different.'" Although the tooling was standard, he installed a slightly larger die with a different shape. Although the product improved, it still broke. He then installed an even larger die and the order ran without mishap. Afterward, Simon commented, "We're taught not to do that," yet mechanically following procedures is no guarantee of a good product either.

Simon's reasoning and actions exemplify the three aspects of common sense in troubleshooting. The operator initially performs a well-established set-up, relying on written procedures, his own memory, or the word of the last operator who handled a similar order. If problems occur, he methodically performs the simplest, most likely adjustments so he can link changes in the product with specific adjustments to run conditions. If by-the-book remedies fail to work, the operator exhibits common sense by changing something. Precisely when this threshold is crossed depends upon the product, the availability of assistance, and the operator's assessment of his ability.

Finally, common sense is demonstrated by the choice of run conditions to vary. In fact, the admonition to "change something, anything" does not really mean *anything*. Some changes, such as in handling hazardous chemicals, are forbidden. More commonly, some actions are viewed as likely remedies, while others are considered implausible solutions.

Beginning with the selection of employees, we have traced a process by which new hires are gradually incorporated into a community of practice. In order to understand how people are transformed into effective workers, this incorporation, as much as any internalization of skills and knowledge, must be understood.

Several features of this process stand out. First, the process is not automatic, nor do operators follow identical trajectories and arrive at identical places in the community of practice. For example, although becoming a master operator is partially a function of longevity, some senior operators remain peripheral. Likewise, there are junior operators who rapidly achieve high visibility and respect among other operators, engineers, and supervisors.

Second, the process of incorporation has a technical basis in running a machine, but operators are immediately exposed to the social and symbolic aspects of production-floor life. Whether by observing their trainers as they interact with other operators, or through conversations and storytelling (Orr 1990), they begin to learn about the distinctions that members of the community attend to. Beginning with minutiae such as numbering systems for reels or product codes, their learning gradually embraces a larger and larger set of distinctions concerning the production floor and its denizens. Gradually, too, they move from being recipients of information about the production floor to enacting some of those very beliefs by their own actions. Ultimately, they help construct the workplace.

We can conclude that the challenge for the operator is more complex than simply learning the basics and then gradually refining his or her technical competency. There is an interpretive basis to production-floor learning, one in which operators ask what is going on and what is expected of them. This interpretive endeavor can be daunting, and we may conceptualize the threats to understanding along the dimensions of consistency and clarity.

Inconsistencies occur between what a trainer or other operator says and what they actually do. They can occur among operators, and they often occur between the pronouncements of supervisors, engineers, or upper managers and their respective actions. As we saw, these inconsistencies are recognized by new operators as a central challenge to their own learning.

The challenge of clarity refers to how explicit production-floor knowledge and skills appear to the novice. We have seen that some procedures and policies are formalized in written documents, but they are necessarily incomplete. Even the message of a memo or remark may be unclear or contentious to the operator. Sometimes, the lack of clarity is blatant, as when an operator refuses to tell another how to perform some task. More commonly, the lack of clarity is unintended, as when an operator declines to impose his or her style on another operator.

We have also seen the importance of incentives for learning. Supervisors may proclaim the skills they wish to see demonstrated, but operators are sensitive to the performances that are read by others as evidence of competence. Just as incentives to pursue different courses of action matter, so does the ability to learn from those actions. We saw evidence of superstitious learning when operators learn lessons that may be incorrect; the pursuit of efficiency and the efficacy of tricks and tinkering are exemplary. Accordingly, the assumption that on-the-job training will provide operators with correct lessons is simplistic.

The picture we have painted in this chapter of the learning challenge faced by new operators is a static one, and in the next chapter we explore how the production floor changes. There we encounter challenges to models of learning in which the workplace is functionally integrated and skill requirements change in consistent ways.

8 REPRODUCTION AND CHANGE

They think it's easy money. They see me with a cup of coffee, not dirty, managing my own time, talking with more people. They assume there's no work to it. But [taps his forehead with a finger] there's lots of thinking, stuff they don't see.
—Operator substituting for his area's vacationing scheduler

In the last chapter we explored how the workplace molds the learning of the new operator. Formal technical training accounts for only part of that learning; the broader lessons taught by the workplace and the gradual incorporation of the newcomer into a community of practice are at least as important.

The new operator is primarily interested in exigencies that could affect her performance at work and how the latter is assessed by others. Despite occasional tales about "the good old days," her attention is on daily concerns; the workplace appears to be timeless. Indeed, from one day to the next the production floor appears remarkably the same, and at the end of fieldwork it seemed to be the same one I had entered ten months earlier. But this continuity must be carefully considered for in large and small ways the production floor was continuously changing. Understanding that process of change is the goal of this chapter, and to do so we shift our attention from the new operator struggling to fit in, to the production floor as a system that changes in complex and sometimes poorly understood ways.

We begin by briefly reviewing some sources of continuity on the production floor that have been introduced in previous chapters. Next, we identify several trends that are changing production work. We explore these through two case studies: the purchase of a new cabling machine and the growing use by some operators of the PRODCON computer system. These cases allow us a preliminary assessment of changes in the operators' role, the tasks they perform, and ultimately the skills they will need. Such assessment is necessarily speculative since it rests on the particular trends identified and their continuation in the future. Thus, conclusions are hedged with the obvious caveats and cautions.

Equally important is a conceptual limitation to the case studies, for they portray the workplace as an integrated system ultimately derived from the logic of the production process. This functional perspective allows us to prognosticate about required future skills, but we must exercise caution here. First, the functional view focuses attention on individual jobs, thereby ignoring organizational worldview and the community of practice. Second, it suggests perhaps more coherence and integration to the workplace than is warranted (Juravich 1985), since the workplace is also a site of tensions that are managed but never fully resolved.

Continuity and Trends

Sources of continuity on the production floor are diverse and many have been touched upon in the previous chapters. New machines have been brought in during the past decades, but few have dramatically changed the operator's engagement with the machine. Operators have been able to build upon their previous skills and knowledge, modifying them slightly in order to adapt to new exigencies.

Organizational regimes have come and gone, but senior operators reported that until recently these had made little impact on the work of running machines. The profiles of good operators and the myths about identifying them have also provided continuity. Tricks and tinkering have long characterized the production floor, and hiring practices have found individuals predisposed to doing so. As discussed in Chapter 7, training serves to communicate the technical skills and knowledge needed to make wire and cable, but it also enculturates operators into a production-floor worldview. The values of individualism and comfort play critical roles in maintaining continuity, for they discourage comparisons and experiments that might lead operators to radically new practices.

Despite the robust sources of continuity, Calhoun Wire and Cable's production floor is today affected by several trends, largely driven by the increased competition discussed in Chapter 6, which are likely to continue to affect production work. A fundamental one is the plant's increasing attention to process improvement. Calhoun Wire and Cable also faces a very tangible spatial problem: Because there is no room for expansion, existing floor space must be made more productive.

The efforts at process improvement are broad in scope and they affect the operators in several ways. Because operators are Engineering's "eyes and ears," they collect data needed to better understand the production process and its variances. Most important, efforts to improve the production process have involved the operators in working on the workplace in order to change the conditions under which wire and cable is produced, rather than simply accepting those conditions.

A related trend is the increased participation by operators in workplace issues, and management's expectation that they are committed to improving the production process. To be sure, operator participation is circumscribed and consists mainly of suggestions to supervisors and engineers. It continues only at the pleasure of management, and it is not institutionalized. Not surprisingly, the demand for operator commitment is not so circumscribed.

The trend toward participation and commitment has increased social interaction among operators, but its impact goes deeper. Operators must increasingly produce performances demonstrating that they are committed and participating workers, rather than just producing wire and cable. These performances allow the company to penetrate previously private spheres of individual identity, for the operator must now act as if he or she were a particular kind of person. Just as process improvement involves operators in producing the workplace they inhabit, participation and commitment demand that they produce a particular identity for at least part of the day.

A third trend is defined by the increasing formalization and standardization of policies and procedures. This trend, too, reflects the drive toward process improvement but also a desire to appear as a rational actor for the benefit of customers (Meyer and Rowan 1977). It places a premium on both oral and written communication, as well as the abilities to collect and analyze data and to compare alternative strategies.

The three preceding trends underlie two others that are perhaps more tangible and noticeable since they involve new technology. The purchase of new production machines that embody microprocessor controls has begun and is expected to continue. These machines generally operate with minimal variance, thereby inverting the present logic that nothing works as it should and the operator is expected to do what it takes to "get product out the door."

The final trend involves the increased use of PRODCON, the firm's computerized information system. PRODCON's terminals are found in each department, and while only a few operators use them, this is expected to increase in the future. Where those terminals are placed and how they are used will profoundly shape work on the production floor.

We turn now to two cases in which these five trends are evident. Both cases concern the adoption of new technology that has affected the operator's work. However, they do not merely study the impacts of new technology on jobs and organization. The adoption of new technology results from organizational choice, and it is used in some ways and not others. It can be a means by which new organizational goals are established, and not simply the means to achieve existing ones (Thomas 1994).

CASE: COMMISSIONING THE TWISTER

The Twister represents a distinct break with Calhoun Wire and Cable's conventional cabling machines. The latter twist the cable components together via the rotation of a large (8–10-foot diameter) bay wheel that holds the individual spools of wire that comprise the cable. The machine output is limited by the revolutions of the bay wheel: 30 to 40 feet per minute is typical.

In contrast, the Twister's pay-off spools remain stationary as the wires are pulled off, drawn together through a die, and then around the take-up reel. There the components are twisted together via the action of a rapidly revolving bow. The entire take-up apparatus can be seen only through a window in the protective chamber that encloses it. The action of the bow allows the Twister to produce 500 feet of cable per minute.

The Twister was purchased as part of a general program to upgrade plant machinery. Calhoun Wire and Cable's European counterpart had purchased the machine, and when an engineer from that plant arrived at Calhoun Wire and Cable to coordinate capital improvements, the Twister provided an obvious starting point. Its speed would allow it to replace two conventional cabling machines.

Introducing the Twister into the plant was coordinated by a team comprised of the Cabling area supervisor, the technician responsible for the machine, and Doyle, a cabling operator. Operators had never joined such a team before, and the importance of the event was signaled when the team flew first to the sister plant to assess the Twister's operation and then to its European manufacturer for a week of training.

According to management, Doyle was included for several reasons. By receiving hands-on training he would subsequently serve as both trainer and resource to his colleagues. His supervisor hoped that by observing the Twister operating in a slightly different setting he would be able to anticipate problems in integrating it into the Cabling area. The engineers hoped Doyle would champion the new machine and sell it to his colleagues upon its arrival. This point is especially important since operators have historically rejected much new machinery. Engineering and management were well aware of the risks in forcing a costly new machine upon the operators. Operator participation on the commissioning team would thus hopefully alleviate two concerns: that the machine would not be fully utilized and that it would be the object of surreptitious tinkering.

When the inspection team returned, Doyle served well as the Twister's champion, and when the machine and its French designer arrived several months later he remained enthusiastic. The commissioning lasted a week during which time Fred, another veteran operator, was trained.

The machine's arrival was watched attentively by everyone in the plant, and a stream of visitors traipsed by to catch a glimpse of it. If the Twister's appearance is striking, its computerized controls are revolutionary. Except for start, stop, and inching (slow speed) buttons, the operator interacts with this new machine via a standard keyboard and cathode ray tube (CRT) built into its main cabinet. The function keys are used to open and close the chamber lid, raise and lower the take-up reel, and start and stop the machine after the power is turned on. The machine is equipped with an alarm bell that indicates faults in the wire being processed, and a printer that records the parameters ("run conditions") the operator selects, any faults encountered during the run, and the actual run conditions when the order is completed.

The operator uses two screens displayed on the CRT to control the machine. The cable parameters screen displays the set of parameters that controls the run. The operator presses the keyboard's directional keys to move from parameter to parameter, and enters values in each field via the numerical keys. The parameters include the outside diameter of the cable, the lay of the completed product, the tension on each pay-off spool, and the linear speed at which the completed cable passes into the take-up chamber. The "splice length" parameter, which allows the operator to stop the machine at a pre-set length, later proved to be critical.

During normal operation, the operator loads an empty reel in the take-up chamber and places the specified spools of component wire on the pay-offs. He threads the latter through the die and into the take-up chamber, where he wraps the cable end around the take-up reel to secure it. He then enters the desired cable parameters, presses the F8 function key, and waits until the machine automatically stops, either because it has come to the splice length he set or because it detected a splice in one of the component wires. He releases the tension on the component wires by pressing another function key, performs a special "nickdown" splice, and then inches the cable about 30 feet forward so that the nickdown splice is firmly wrapped around the take-up reel. Then he resets the tensions, types in a new splice length, and presses F8.

The second screen is the cable library screen which allows the user to store the parameters for over three hundred products. Whenever the same product identification number is entered by the operator, the saved parameters are automatically used.

The Twister presents the operator with feedback about its performance. Messages flash on the CRT and alarm bells ring to alert the operator about conditions such as a misaligned take-up reel, broken or faulty pay-off wire, an incorrectly positioned chamber lid, or the end of a length of cable. The operator silences the alarm at the keyboard, but the machine is inoperative until the problem is corrected.

The Twister has had a profound and immediate effect on cabling work. First, the cost of the machine mitigates against tinkering. The inspection team initially proposed adding a dancer, but the chief engineer denied the request: "You don't go tinkering with something you paid over $300,000 for." Other suggestions were made, but only one was approved: X's were painted on the pay-off wheels so their rotation would be obvious and less hazardous.

Second, unlike older cablers, the Twister is a finely balanced machine with precise tolerances. It is the proverbial "tightly coupled machine" in which variances in one part have consequences elsewhere. An engineer noted that an operator can usually find ways to run a machine faster to increase output, "but [with the Twister] he may also be putting a load on a bearing that's so finely balanced it can be damaged. The operator probably doesn't even know about the bearing." This reinforced the ban on tinkering, although the possibility of formally approved modifications was left open. These have followed a formal decision-making process based on data collection, generation of written specifications and drawings, discussion in meetings, and consensus as to the desired outcomes. Operators have been closely involved in this process, but unauthorized modifications remain forbidden. In fact, all modifications are approved by the machine's manufacturer, both for expert advice and to maintain the machine's warranty.

Third, the machine's speed dramatically affects the pacing of work. Because many orders can be processed in less than five minutes, the operator may have insufficient time to complete paperwork and prepare the next order. This requires that he perform these tasks with the machine idle, thereby breaking a production floor taboo.

The Twister's speed also allows it to rapidly produce scrap. If an operator errs in loading a conventional cabler and corrects his/her mistake within a few minutes, less than a hundred feet of scrap is produced. In contrast, the Twister can ruin an entire order within several minutes. The fear of "running scrap" places a premium on carefully inspecting the component wires and verifying paperwork. "Everything has to be right before you start," commented Fred. Doyle and Fred both commented that they developed more meticulous routines for inspecting and verifying paperwork, tasks which were accentuated by the unfamiliar keyboard controls.

The Twister's safety interlocks and alarm signals pose a special challenge. The need to set cable parameters imposes rigid requirements on the operator, but the sequence in which parameters are met varies. For example, the operator must set a splice length, but this may be the first, second, or third parameter he or she enters. While the machine's interlocks prevent operation until the required parameters are set, this does not ensure a successful run. Specifically, when the operator releases the tension on the pay-off spools in order to make a nickdown, the machine does not prompt him/her to reset them when done. Operators fear they will forget to do so, causing the cable to disintegrate in the protective take-up chamber.

It is this combination of rigid run conditions that must be set, the arbitrariness of their entry into the machine, the lack of opportunity to perform adjustments during a run, and the risk of catastrophic oversights that create the operator's challenge: to develop a routine to efficiently produce good product without causing, as Fred remarked, "the damn signal to ring."

Another innovation is that the Twister produces a written history. Scant attention was paid initially to the paper tapes produced during each run. Soon the unambiguous, permanent records were used to establish what *really* happened to an order, where such certitude was previously impossible. Within a week, the Cabling supervisor spoke of "hitting" other supervisors with the tapes in meetings.

Despite its impressive capabilities, operators soon discovered a difficulty in using the Twister. The pay-off device incorporates a sensor that automatically stops the machine when it detects a splice in the component wire. Engineers planned to use this capability so the operator could perform the required nickdown splice. However, when running at high speeds, the splice enters the take-up chamber, forcing the operator to lean awkwardly into it to make the splice.

Fred and Doyle attempted to anticipate splices by using the length stickers affixed by the Packing operators to each spool of wire. They set the splice length parameter for a length just short of the expected splice location: The resulting "cushion" allowed them to then slowly inch the cable ahead to find the splice before it entered the chamber. However, keeping track of lengths posed a formidable task.

Both operators soon developed strategies for running the Twister. We begin with Fred as he prepares to run a "twisted pair" of wires (i.e., a cable of two components). He removes the length stickers from each spool after loading them and sticks them to the workbench. They list the footage of each length of wire on each pay-off spool:

PAY-OFF SPOOL #1		PAY-OFF SPOOL #2	
1	4090	1	975
2	2710	2	3630
3	3700	3	1000
		4	514
		5	710
		6	3300
		7	371
	10,500		10,500

Since the last lengths (#3 and #7, respectively) will be the first to pay off the spools, the first nickdown should be made at 371 feet. Using the keyboard, Fred sets the splice length for 340 feet, giving him a 31-foot cushion. He sets the speed at 500 feet per minute and starts the machine. The machine stops in less than a minute and Fred releases the pay-off tensions. He inches the cable ahead until he finds the splice at 369 feet and performs the specified nickdown.

Fred inspects the length stickers again and notes that length #6 on Pay-off #2 will end before he reaches the end of length #3 on Pay-off #1. Thus, he subtracts his 30-foot cushion from 3300 feet and sets the splice length for 3270 feet. He sets the speed for 500 feet per minute and the tensions on the pay-offs, and starts the machine. It stops within five minutes, and again Fred inches the cable forward, finds the splice, and performs the nickdown.

He uses an electronic calculator to compute the next splice length. He enters "371 + 3300," and the calculator displays "3671." Fred finds he is nearly to the end of length #3 on Pay-off #1, so he inches the cable forward 29 feet until he finds the splice and performs the nickdown. Because 29 feet is below the minimal acceptable length, he subtracts it from 710 feet, the footage of the next good length on either pay-off; the calculator indicates 681 feet. He subtracts the cushion allowing for any error on the length sticker, sets the splice length for 651 feet, and starts the Twister.

Doyle disliked calculating splice lengths and occasionally lost his place in the calculations. "It's just the number of splices and high speeds. Sooner or later you'll forget." Once, after losing his place in the calculations, Doyle tried a different way to run the machine. He lowered the speed to 250 feet per minute, set the total cable length and splice length the same, and started the machine. This allowed the fault detector to automatically stop the machine at a splice. By trial and error, Doyle determined the maximum speed at which the splice would stop before entering the chamber. Thus, by using lower speeds, Doyle avoided the calculations entailed in anticipating splices, although he worried that his style failed to use the full speed of the Twister.

Within a week, Fred and Doyle had settled upon two distinct styles of operation, each claiming his was best. Several operators opined that Fred's was the "smarter" one, since it required more calculations, and they knew that Doyle's had been born out of his inability to perform the calculations. Finally, an order that ran during two shifts allowed the contrasting styles to be evaluated, and Doyle's method proved more productive, at least for spools with many splices. Soon Fred and Doyle were using Doyle's method if the pay-off spools had more than five or six splices, while they still performed calculations if there were fewer. Months later, the problem was resolved when management ordered that all spools sent to the Twister contain only one continuous length of wire. The need to calculate vanished.

In terms of the labor process debate (Thompson 1983), Doyle's strategy is deskilling while Fred's is upskilling, although neither operator conceptualized his actions as such. Doyle saw his strategy as the easier one, and understood that the capability of the Twister to stop automatically had been purchased and would ultimately be utilized. Fred saw performing the calculations as necessary in order to keep the machine running. Still, Fred's style conserved operator skills on the production floor rather than exporting them to a computer algorithm, the emerging locus of many former skills.

In summary, the case of the Twister reveals an important consequence of process improvement: The purchase of new technology can alter how operators engage their machines and thus can transform the traditional basis of their practice. Operator participation assumed new importance, and indeed the commissioning of the Twister served as a stage for some operators to demonstrate their competence and to enhance their reputations. In fact, Doyle's reputation suffered from the perception that he was unable to perform the required calculations. Participation thus made it difficult to hide from the scrutiny of others.

The trend of standardization and formalization manifested itself in several ways. Although Fred and Doyle experimented with the machine, ultimately this gave way to written, formalized procedures. And while operators participated in discussions about the Twister, the days of the "Corporate Rambo" or "John Wayne" were long gone: Action followed collective deliberations and decision making. Most dramatically, the Twister effected standardized run conditions via its library function. Styles became stored on floppy diskettes, and while the operator could override them, this too was recorded and left the operator vulnerable if a problem with an order arose.

The Twister's computerized controls also changed the operator's engagement with the machine. Many traditional sensory cues vanished, and the operators experienced a disjunction between the entry of abstract cable parameters and their physical referents. The Twister also eliminated the variances underlying the need to learn about individual machines.

It is also striking that the commissioning constituted a period of instability in which ways of working were examined, challenged, and evaluated. Rather than following a clearly defined set of task requirements, the operators were involved in shaping which tasks would become standard, and thus which skills would be exercised. Social status and individual reputations became entangled with evaluating alternatives, and assessment of styles as smart or dumb came to reflect judgments about the operators who proposed them.

CASE: USING PRODCON

PRODCON is not a production machine but rather the automated production control system used by Calhoun Wire and Cable. When the factory receives an order, PRODCON is used to determine its components, the steps in their manufacture, and the length of time it will take to make them. The system is also used to keep track of the reels of products as they pass through the production floor, and it is this capacity that directly affects the operators: PRODCON can be used to locate missing reels of wire, to determine deadlines for processing them, or to replace lost documentation.

PRODCON is accessed through the computer terminals located in each department. The terminals display specialized screens, each of which contains information about an order from the time it is received until it is shipped to the customer. Few of Calhoun Wire and Cable's operators use more than a handful of the many screens available, and the interaction between employee and PRODCON is restricted through electronic codes. For example, most operators can only call up and read a few screens, and they cannot enter data into them.

Operators received training when PRODCON was first introduced, but there was unanimous agreement that the training was inadequate and that the system was largely irrelevant to daily work. Even today, there is no comprehensive PRODCON user's manual and most operators who use the system keep photocopies of a few screens with handwritten notes to guide them. In most areas, one or two operators are able to use PRODCON and they are usually willing to perform this service for their colleagues. This ability is rewarded on performance reviews, and even more important, these operators are frequently selected to substitute for their department's allocators and schedulers (administrative support staff) during their vacations. A tacit career ladder off the production floor is developing and operators who gravitate toward the computer have an advantage in climbing it.

Supervisors encourage operators to learn about PRODCON. They speak of these operators as being more inquisitive than others, being able to get along well with people, and being more responsible and trustworthy. While these assessments clearly benefit some operators, others are concerned that the resulting transfers are siphoning good people off the production floor. The Packing Department scheduler, for example, is widely respected and was promoted from the production floor. However, many operators commented that the loss of her knowledge from the production floor weakened the latter and situated more power "on the other side" (i.e., in the administrative offices).

Many operators believe that the future of the production floor and the security of their jobs depends on the placement and use of computers, PRODCON or otherwise, on it. To be sure, many of these same operators view this development with trepidation. Some identify themselves as "mechanical people" and others take pride in the craft basis of their work. Many have deliberately avoided employment in the region's many electronics firms, preferring "real" manufacturing work instead. Still, they are clearly aware of the computer's potential to improve the production process and they are resigned to their presence in the plant. While a few operators refuse to learn to use them, the vast majority see them as necessary, and they voice concerns that computers will be placed on the administrative side of the plant and not on the production floor itself. This, they fear, will further rob the production floor of talented workers and ultimately erode the basis for operator power. In the extreme, they fear that the plant will end up completely in the hands of people who have never seen, much less made, the very product they control.

The one department where all operators routinely interact with PRODCON is the Stocking Department. These operators are responsible for storing and moving reels of product through the plant, and for maintaining the electronic records about their location and status. The impact of PRODCON on the two Shipping area operators within the Stocking Department illustrates the potential influence of PRODCON on work.

The Shipping operators prepare orders of product that are sent to Techno Industries' shipping facility and then to individual customers. The operators verify that any required tests or inspections have been performed, and they perform the routine paperwork and "terminal work" needed to "close" an order and prepare it for shipping. They also resolve any discrepancies between an order's records and the actual product.

Jeff and Alan, the Shipping operators, begin each day by reviewing the stacks of paperwork for the wire and cable to be shipped. They verify the data on each form for consistency and sense (e.g., that the correct units of measurement are used or the size of the order is plausible), and then they log on to PRODCON where they update each record. They do this by entering codes and data into several screens that electronically "move" the order from the plant to the delivery truck. For example, Jeff views a screen that shows the quantity of each product and finds 157,000 feet "on hand." This corresponds to the 157,000 feet he is shipping out. He deducts that quantity from the screen, thereby instructing the PRODCON database that all the material has been shipped. For each order, he calls up several different screens and updates each one prior to shipping the order.

After updating the database, Jeff searches for inconsistencies in the record. For example, he calls up the screen showing the location of the 157,000-foot order he just shipped, and it correctly indicates "no location." There would be a problem if a location had been indicated, since Jeff had just closed the order on another screen.

Resolving discrepancies between records and orders is a constant chore, so troubleshooting is a daily activity. It is generally quite routine but often requires extensive sleuthing, visits to offices throughout the plant, and even searches of the plant areas before problems can be resolved. Other problems require discussions with sales representatives or other employees. For example, Alan found an order for 100,000 feet of wire, but 105,000 feet had been produced. Alan had to ascertain whether the sales representative wanted to try to sell the excess wire to the customer, store it on the production floor, or destroy it.

Alan and Jeff had worked in other areas of Stocking before PRODCON arrived and they felt it had clearly affected the tasks they performed. Meticulous data entry and verification, while always important, were now at a premium. Both remarked that their jobs required people who were inquisitive and who would take initiative.

They also discussed the need to develop several routines for processing orders without losing their place. The patterned way in which they would check the status of a recently updated order on several screens exemplifies such routines. They said that mistakes were inevitable without routines and the discipline to follow them, and both spoke of the pride they took in their reputation for accuracy.

Alan and Jeff also discussed the need to develop several conceptual models of the plant and the production process. Unlike operators who focus their attention on an area or machine, these operators must understand the likely flow of various products through the entire production process. They need detailed knowledge of, as one put it, "the hiding places" in the plant, as well as friends in all areas to call on for assistance. They need to understand the functions of the various administrative departments, and the special expertise of individuals throughout the plant. Last, they developed a model of PRODCON itself as a symbolic system with various logical connections that could be used to troubleshoot problems.

Despite concerns that PRODCON will over time drain talent from the production floor, in the short term many credit it with changing the balance of power between the production floor and the administrative departments. Previously, production control was achieved through written documentation. While orders were scheduled in accordance with explicit policies, sales representatives, planners, and other higher-status employees frequently tried to move their orders ahead in the queue either to please a customer or to cover up their own poor planning. PRODCON changed this by providing unambiguous estimates of the time to produce each product and by making product records accessible to everyone. Many users of the system noted that it has imposed conformity to rules by making tampering visible: Witnesses are always watching.

In general, PRODCON has increased communication within the plant, and this has further transformed Alan and Jeff's work. Much of their communication must be handled with tact. During one interview, Jeff declared that it was time to deal with a planner who he felt had been ignoring a problem. The customer had originally ordered 200,000 feet of wire and then reduced the order to 195,000 feet. But the planner never advised the production floor, which correctly produced the original amount. Jeff had asked the planner to resolve the issue with the customer, and suspected that he was avoiding the issue since it reflected poorly on him. He would visit the planner and tactfully provoke a decision. He explained that he and Alan could use "the big stick" and embarrass people, but this then exposes them to retaliation in unknown ways. They had concluded that a low-key, "we're in this together" approach was ultimately more effective. Still, they distributed a monthly list of unresolved orders that identified the responsible planners.

Alan and Jeff clearly recognized their power to force issues as well as the limits on exercising their power. They were often frustrated with the spools of wire and cable cluttering their area, but they were committed to using tact, reminders, and their capacity to perform favors to resolve problems. And while they recognized that the skills their jobs required have changed, they said the most important qualification was to be responsible people who stayed as late as necessary to process an order.

SKILLS REVISITED

We may now summarize how the trends we have identified affect Calhoun Wire and Cable's production workers. This assessment is incomplete since the transformation of the production floor has only just begun and it has affected some areas more than others. Nevertheless, some preliminary judgments can be made.

First, new machines may remove the operator from direct tactile involvement with the product and decrease the importance of learning about the idiosyncratic characteristics of each machine. The process performed by the machine becomes defined by a set of symbols, sometimes with unclear physical referents. These changes in engagement with the machine in turn affect learning. Where formerly an operator could learn to start and stop a cabling machine, and then gradually sharpen his performance by running it, considerable training is required before ever operating the Twister. Learning is moved, as one operator commented, "up front" and is based increasingly on mastery of documentation than on the extant oral tradition. The chief manufacturing engineer anticipated more algorithmic procedures and development of a generic set of machine control skills that would be readily transferable throughout the plant.

Second, visualization of the workplace as a system—the "big picture"—is supported. The commissioning of the Twister required that operators pay attention to the routes by which spools of wire entered and left the machine, and it served as an occasion for considerable exploration of the workplace. PRODCON, too, provides an abstract model of the entire production process that is accessible to anyone. Significantly, this model is of limited use without a clear understanding of the physical layout of the plant and the work of other people in it.

A corollary here is that as the big picture becomes increasingly salient, it becomes more difficult to ascertain the specific skills and knowledge needed to perform that work. Seemingly irrelevant information about administrative departments, other areas, and specific individuals can suddenly be useful. Operators who interacted with PRODCON were widely known as ones to go to for information, and they had reputations as operators who were always trying to find out more about the plant.

Third, operators are increasingly working with information, as well as with machines. Process improvement is based on data collection, but its implications go further. Operators are called on to represent data via words, numbers, drawings, and tables, and, increasingly, to utilize engineering documentation such as specification control drawings.

As operators manipulate more information, they assume more responsibility for detecting errors or discrepancies. Their work thus becomes more "detail-oriented," as many remarked. At the same time that they are grounded in details, they are asked to speculate about the consequences of pursuing different courses of action, to systematically test hypotheses about production problems, and to develop an attitude of skepticism about seemingly self-evident facts. Accordingly, they are asked to doubt their experiences in the workplace and to adopt a questioning attitude toward much that had been taken for granted.

Fourth, social skills that allow interactions with people from diverse departments have become important. Few operators today remain firmly in one area, focusing their attention only on "their" machines. Cross-training contributes to this, and more and more daily work is conducted in the context of a larger production-floor system. The ability to communicate with operators from other areas, with representatives from administrative offices (who see themselves as higher-status), with engineers, and even with vendors and customers, is now expected. Much operator participation involves collective inputs to decisions, conducted at meetings in which public speaking is expected and a written record is produced. Comments that were formerly made privately to friends, and that could later be denied, have moved into the public domain, where they leave a permanent record.

Finally, work is changing in ways that affect not just skills and knowledge but an operator's identity and his or her relationship to Calhoun Wire and Cable. Participation itself is a double-edged sword. To be sure, it permits or demands the operator to be more engaged in the affairs of the workplace, but it also allows the latter to be more involved in the life of the operator. No longer can an operator simply "do his time" each day, caring little about the quality of the product produced or the inefficiency of his own work habits. Instead, he must increasingly be perceived as the kind of person who is committed and willing to participate. We have seen that operators must create projects, defend their ideas, negotiate with others in the workplace, and generally act as advocates for themselves. This change involves new and different required skills, but it goes further: It entails a new and different sort of identity for the operator.

WORLDVIEW

The preceding picture of skills, although necessarily speculative, is based on trends that are already transforming Calhoun Wire and Cable. Yet these trends do not just affect job skills, for they change an organizational worldview and community of practice as well. This makes predicting the impact of change even more difficult since the operators' interpretations of work and workplace are involved.

The traditional conception of the individual that emphasized comfort, personal style, and privacy is gradually changing. This respect for the individual served to insulate the operator from deeper demands by the company. In effect, operators sold their bundle of skills, but their identities remained inviolate.

On today's production floor, such individualism is harder to maintain. Individual styles are increasingly assessed, and actions and their rationales are publicly debated. Operators today participate collectively in decision making, thus limiting their capacity to go their own ways. Tinkering, which has often been a solitary, surreptitious activity, is being curtailed and replaced by participation in officially sanctioned projects. Public discussion and permanent records of decisions further reduce the previously cherished privacy of the operator, and the traditional avenues for self-expression are increasingly blocked.

Working on the workplace via projects does, however, offer new opportunities for demonstrating skills and knowledge. Although historically individualism has been valued, it has been narrowly conceived. In an era of participation, previously ignored capabilities of workers become salient and can be expressed: drawing diagrams, composing letters, leading meetings, bargaining with coworkers, and so on. What is less certain, however, is the extent to which the company will require that operators demonstrate these previously irrelevant skills. Clearly though, the operator's opportunity to express them is accompanied by the expectation that he or she will do so.

The effect of participation on the individual is thus complex. Operators speak of the need to perform in ways that demonstrate that they are committed people, and the need to present such performances is an intrusion into previously protected regions of the self. In this sense, Calhoun Wire and Cable sees itself as hiring distinct people, and not just the capabilities to perform tasks. This simultaneously acknowledges the uniqueness of the person and allows the company to penetrate more deeply the previously private realms of that person.

The growing differentiation of the community of practice also challenges traditional conceptions of production-floor society. Veteran operators recounted how they formerly interacted primarily with operators from their own department, whereas today they routinely interact with a diverse array of actors, including administrators, engineers, and customers.

The social universe has changed in other ways, too. Newly hired operators are generally better educated, more comfortable with computers, and eager to learn about the plant. The growing importance of training and projects provides new tasks and roles for operators, as well as opportunities to enhance reputations. Previously, operators were known by how well they ran their machines, but now there are operators whose technical expertise is unspectacular, but who nonetheless are respected as trainers or for their ability to organize projects. As production-floor tasks increase, it also becomes harder to envision a single profile of the good operator: There are now more idiosyncratic ways to fulfill the role.

The professionalization of the supervisors is also salient here. Supervision is based less on technical expertise, and so operators are performing for a critical but somewhat naive audience. Previously, they knew their supervisors had been one of them, but this is not true today. Job ladders have also been truncated, and operators openly wonder what is to happen to their own careers.

Assumptions about human nature, too, may well be challenged. Traditionally, explanations for an operator's actions have been couched in terms of what is natural for an operator to do under specific circumstances. But those circumstances tacitly reflect how operators are assigned to machines, how their performances are evaluated, and how they are rewarded. These practices are changing and what is "natural" can no longer be assumed.

The relationship between operator and the environment is changing as the factors relevant to the operator's work expand and become more complex. Database systems such as PRODCON are supporting an expanded view of the workplace. For those operators conversant with it, PRODCON allows them to see previously obscure relationships between areas, as well as how their work is part of the overall production process. Coupled with the emphasis on projects that allows operators to inquire about the plant, an expanded conception of the relevant environment is gradually being developed. Cross-training just reinforces this larger perspective on the workplace.

Simultaneously, however, the operator's view of the machines she or he runs is being obscured. The ban on tinkering, sometimes reflected in seals and locks on machine housings, prevents operators from looking into forbidden domains and makes the machine a "black box" that communicates via inputs and outputs. The operator's view of the environment is thus enlarged and in many ways enriched, but an important part of it—exploring the workings of machines—is less accessible. Rather than tinker with new machines, operators must learn how they work and conform to the constraints they impose.

Participation in projects changes a fundamental relationship between operator and environment. Before, operators contributed relatively little to designing or producing the workplace, except through tinkering. However, tinkering is ad hoc and done in response to the plans and purchases of others in the workplace. Projects, on the other hand, formally involve operators in producing the workplace. Ironically, the price operators pay is that they must abandon efforts to modify the workplace privately.

Insofar as the production process is improved, the conception of the environment will likely be affected. Historically, the environment has been conceptualized as only partially under human understanding or control. As we have seen, operators believe temperature, drafts, and humidity affect their machines in mysterious ways, and that identical machine settings can lead to vastly different outcomes under different environmental conditions. All this changes as systematic data collection clarifies the conditions affecting machines and products, and much of the mystery of making wire and cable may vanish.

Accordingly, the conversation between art and science is changing. Subjective judgments, such as the clarity of a mark or the softness of a flame, will undoubtedly remain part of the operator's repertoire, but many variables will be better controlled by the operator, so that making wire and cable becomes more of a science than an art.

The transformation of the environment is also eroding common sense as the basis for all actions in the workplace. This has been treated as a quality of individual operators, who either possessed or lacked it. Yet what is logical or self-evident depends on the environment in which actions are contemplated, and that environment is more complex now. Previously, operators demonstrated common sense by setting up their orders according to standard practice. The latter included some written procedures, but as we have seen, such procedures are generally guidelines, there are stylistic variations, and much information is transmitted orally. As styles are compared and optimal ones selected, standard practices become explicit and formalized. The operator who fails to heed them no longer lacks common sense but rather is disregarding instructions.

Another facet of common sense, the admonition to change something if problems persist, is more difficult to follow when tricks and tinkering are under scrutiny. Understanding the process is difficult when operators can "change anything," and now there is a greater emphasis on systematically disentangling how run conditions affect products. The resulting knowledge underlies improving the process, but it does so through systematic data collection that is the scourge of the "lone wolf" operator changing anything.

Finally, the orientation to time is changing. Many operators have historically viewed their connection to the plant as temporary, protecting themselves by making no commitment to it. But projects take months or years to complete, and this compels many operators to reassess their relationship with the firm. This is not to say that all operators are committed; many remain aloof and others depart. However, most who remain speak of things to be done months in the future or of the long-term future of the plant, something quite foreign before.

Time is also becoming institutionalized in a historical record so that the past is less deniable. Public meetings with written records, hard copies available from computerized information systems, and tapes spewed out of new machines all contribute to the creation of a production-floor history. Ideas suggested, errors made, and public proclamations live on and may be retrieved and used to support diverse agendas. The workplace thus remembers more, and it may forget and forgive less.

CONTESTS AND CONTRADICTIONS

Our exploration of the production-floor worldview and community of practice enlarges our understanding of how several trends are affecting the work of operators. The analysis presented, however, assumes that the workplace is well-integrated so that changes in one part have predictable effects elsewhere. This confidence in functional integration may be misplaced, for planned changes sometimes have unintended consequences that pose new challenges to workers. Alternatively, some projects are based on seemingly contradictory values, each consistent with a different organizational worldview. The workplace is thus a site of tensions that make confident and precise predictions about the future problematical.

A first set of tensions concerns management's effort to minimize variances in processing wire and cable. This challenge enjoys widespread support, and no one publicly opposes developing a better production process. Nonetheless, minimizing variances has complex ramifications for the community of practice. As we have seen, controlling variances is associated with prohibiting tricks and tinkering, and reducing operator discretion through formalized procedures and the purchase of better machinery. All these changes erode the historical basis of pride on the production floor, a quality that both operators and management agree has been critical to the company's success. Because variance underlies pride, we may speculate that the quest to eliminate variance may be more rewarding to operators than its ultimate success, which will greatly reduce their autonomy.

Another set of tensions concerns the values of individualism and collectivism. We have seen that individual comfort and the right to privacy have been paramount. The company has intruded little into the recesses of a person's identity and instead asked only that they run their machines. The cost has been the inability to compare run conditions, which in turn permitted suboptimal operator styles to persist.

This, too, is changing. Operators have gained more input into workplace issues, but this is exercised in formalized projects. Important decisions are collective in nature, and so while operators collectively may have more input to decisions, the decision making of individual operators is curtailed. Again, the tradition of comfort is maintained insofar as suboptimal styles persist and attempts to improve the process are minimal.

A related tension involves the assessment of operators, and the extent to which they are expected to perform similarly. As the range of tasks assigned to operators increases, the skills required expand accordingly. There is a tension between management's predilection for assessing the performance of operators along the same profile of required skills, and accepting the possibility of a multitude of incomparable but equally valuable profiles of skills. The choice is between a production floor populated by identically skilled operators who vary only slightly in their mastery of the same skills, and one with a mosaic of idiosyncratically skilled operators.

The distinction between working in and working on the workplace entails additional tensions, for the very definition of work is being questioned. The tradition of working in the workplace meant that operator ideas were devalued, but the demands made on them were minimal. Many senior operators said that they had remained at their machines for years, paying minimal attention to the quality of their work or the activities of others around them. They could point out the foibles of engineers and supervisors and critique their plans for the workplace precisely because their own ideas were not solicited. The irony today is that because they are expected to share their ideas, there are few excuses for not pursuing them. The cost of being heard is thus the greater penetration by the company into what was previously the individual's personal and private life.

More mundane issues exacerbate this tension. Despite the emphasis on projects, time to work on them is often unavailable in the operator's schedule. Participation requires time, and the increasing movement toward "just in time" manufacturing, also a hallmark of the rational production process, reduces the time available for discussions. Other issues concern the increase in formal meetings and the operator's greater involvement in information management. Both these trends conflict with the desire of many operators, especially senior ones, to "get back to work" running their machines.

Finally, the professionalization of supervision creates a tension that affects operators. These supervisors have not been promoted from the production floor and they are often less technically knowledgeable than their more experienced operators. Despite the operators' frustrations, the gaps in a supervisor's technical competence permit the operator greater freedom. Supervisors of the past may have been prepared to answer any question, but they were equally ready with commands.

The professionalization of supervision has also removed a traditional job ladder for operators precisely at a time when more educated and ambitious operators are being hired. Ultimately, such operators may stagnate and move elsewhere, seek out career opportunities elsewhere in Calhoun Wire and Cable or in Techno Industries, or they may simply adjust to their fate. Finding ways to retain the better operators the company works so hard to hire, along with maintaining pride in their workmanship, will probably remain issues for the foreseeable future.

Conclusion

The discussion in this chapter reminds us that the new operator enters a dynamic workplace that is changing in complex ways. Some changes are minute and constant, and they may not even be perceived as such by denizens of the production floor. Others are dramatic and precipitous, with immediate effects on daily work.

Even where evidence of trends that affect work can be identified, their effects on organizational worldview and community of practice may be difficult to anticipate except in the most general terms. Many operators are aware of these trends and they adjust their behavior accordingly; the willingness to accept computers on the production floor is exemplary. In general, however, operators respond to the very specific demands, both large and small, that affect their daily work. Their responses to new demands are partially formed through discussions, but variation in response is the norm. Some carry their performance reviews in their pockets as evidence of their betrayal by a heartless company, and others claim that they enjoy coming to work for the first time in years. Most remain ambivalent, supporting some changes such as the purchase of new state-of-the-art machines, and resisting others, like the ban on tinkering with those very machines.

Our analysis suggests that we must be careful in confining ourselves to a functional model of the workplace. This model is seductive, since it allows us to trace the impact of change upon individual job skills: As tasks and roles change, required skills follow accordingly. These newly required skills fit together and create new but unambiguous demands upon workers. Required skills are thus conceptualized as discrete variables that may change in value, but their interactions are not problematical.

While useful for sketching the broadest contours of change in the workplace, the functional perspective is limited in important ways. It traces the effects of change directly upon individual jobs, and not upon the community of practice and production-floor worldview, although the latter are being dramatically transformed.

The changes we have seen affect more than bundles of required job skills: They affect the identities of workers too. The relationships among skills, too, may be critical. For example, the attention of operators is being drawn in different directions as they are required to pay attention simultaneously to details *and* the big picture. How this will be resolved remains to be seen.

Finally, the workplace we experience is less a stable, functionally integrated system than it is a concatenation of forces in a dynamic equilibrium. Such a system can suddenly become quite different from what it is, and predicting its future is uncertain at best. The danger of hubris looms large in such a world.

9 CONCLUSION

What's happened to tricks and tinkering here?
—the anthropologist

You mean tampering. Tampering, that's what they call it here.
—senior Extruding operator [grinning widely]

Several years after fieldwork in Calhoun Wire and Cable ended, the company established a smaller facility called NewSite. It provides a suitable conclusion to our workplace excursions, and so we pay a cursory visit to NewSite in order to see how work is changing in Calhoun's "workplace of the future." Our visit complete, we return to the concept of skill requirements that launched our journey, and we conclude with some final thoughts on workplaces and learning.

NewSite

NewSite employs several dozen operators who transferred from Calhoun Wire and Cable to manufacture a single product line. Its goals are to reduce the costs of production by at least one-third and to reduce the lead time to produce an order from thirty to six days. NewSite was established as a model for future development in Calhoun and is expected to be a destination for potential customers ("tourists") wishing to see Techno's manufacturing prowess on display.

The plant has introduced several organizational and technological innovations. Standardization of the production process is of paramount importance in NewSite and its ramifications are widespread. Tinkering with machines and the use of sundry tricks are strictly forbidden so that reliable data can be collected. Operators spend hours brainstorming ideas about the run conditions that affect product characteristics, and the effects of many of these have been compared through controlled experiments. A supervisor commented, "You can't get away with 'gut feeling' anymore. It's got to be based on data." Many tricks have been shown to be unnecessary or even counterproductive, and products are run on standard settings arrived at by consensus. The operator may perform some adjustments during a run if necessary, but she or he must pull out of the order and notify her team leader if these prove unsuccessful.

Standardization has effected changes in an operator's use of reasoning and problem solving. Individual machines were formerly the objects of such activities, but now it is the production process that must be understood and improved. Supervisors and operators indicated no dramatic increase in the level of skills required to do this, but some operators nonetheless found it exceedingly difficult to redirect their efforts.

Operators have extended discussion and standardization into domains previously deemed private. "Grabbing gravy," for example, has long been a source of conflict among operators, especially those on different shifts. The practice refers to searching for "long hits" (lengthy orders) instead of short ones, since these reduce the number of machine set-ups an operator performs. When a dispute about grabbing gravy arose in NewSite, operators held a meeting and discovered that their individual definitions of long and short hits varied. They ultimately agreed on the lengths that count as long and short hits in NewSite.

Standardization of production has had a paradoxical effect on job skills. If we focus on operating a machine, it translates into routinized work, and ultimately, more homogeneously skilled operators. In the extreme, each operator becomes cross-trained into the standardized procedures of all areas. Involvement in understanding and improving the production process, however, has a contrary effect. Because that process is complex, understanding it provides numerous opportunities for operators to exercise their unique talents. Some are filling leadership roles, others have an affinity for using Statistical Processing Control ("SPC") techniques and experiments, and still others generate new forms and documents. Some operators remain the masters of craft-like skills, while others serve as culture brokers between areas. As machine operation becomes more routinized, operators may thus become heterogeneously skilled, mastering sophisticated analytical, communication, and social skills. The potential to do this, however, depends on management's continuing commitment to operator participation in process improvement.

In order to achieve standardization and to obtain the willingness of operators to comply with it, a variety of teams has been instituted. These complement the facility's traditional functional areas and managerial positions. Team membership is voluntary and many individuals belong to several teams. Operators are members of all teams except one responsible for long-term factory planning. Even that team solicits operator input about new technology since it wants to avoid the "white elephants"—machines bought with little thought as to how they fit into the production process—which occasionally appear in Calhoun Wire and Cable. Compensation, performance reviews, discipline, and scheduling are the only issues from which operators are excluded.

Each functional area has a team of operators that assesses ideas for resolving problems or modifying machinery. The capacity of such teams to act is constrained by routing all requests to modify machines through a single shop foreman. The presence of other teams with cross-functional responsibilities also exerts a powerful influence. A pillar of the new philosophy is "synergy," by which actions are planned, implemented, assessed, and modified across all areas. The ultimate goal is to optimize *factory* productivity rather than that of individual areas.

Supervisors and operators concurred that cooperation and the ability to work in groups is extremely important in NewSite. Several operators commented that the major obstacle to synergy is the occasional lack of tolerance for other viewpoints. Others remarked that some people have been unable or unwilling to adapt to the plant's new "organizational culture."

Systematic training has become more important due to standardization. Operators have engaged in extensive discussions that culminated in step-by-step flowcharts for performing many tasks. These charts are the outcome of a process in which discrete styles are described, compared, and evaluated, and ultimately a single procedure is prescribed. Alternative elements of style have been experimentally assessed, and their effects on products throughout the plant have been traced. Just as standardization of run conditions removed gut feeling as a rationale for choice, so flowcharts have removed the operator's traditional right to "comfort."

Pages of plastic-sheathed flowcharts adorn most machines, available to any operator as needed, but most operators claim they are too complex to use. A single box of an elaborate Extruding area flowchart, for example, is decomposed into seventeen discrete steps. Operators and management alike acknowledged that the greatest value of the flowcharts is in their development: Operators learn that they perform the same tasks in different ways, and that some of these ways vary in their consequences. Still, as an Extruding operator opined, "Flowcharting alone is suicide."

The adoption of "just in time" (JIT) manufacturing principles has also affected training by speeding up production and minimizing the queues of products between functional areas. Because products proceed rapidly through the plant, some operators may move to several different areas each day, greatly increasing the importance of cross-training. Flowcharts are used in such training, and each area has its formal checklists of tasks the newcomer must master. Standardized peer training conforming to the "classroom" model described in Chapter 7 thus occurs "up front," before the operator touches the machine.

The domain of training has expanded as engineers and supervisors instruct operators in analytical methods to improve the production process. These include training in conducting meetings and designing experiments, and more broadly, the approach of Total Quality Management. SPC techniques such as flowcharting, histograms, Pareto diagrams, and control charts have become especially important. Operators generally collect data for and interpret the results of the techniques, with most calculations performed by an engineer.

The plant also incorporates many technologies that affect work. Reels of product are transported by pneumatic pallet jacks, and power pay-off and take-up devices also make handling heavy reels easier. Spooling machines have been ergonomically redesigned to reduce stress, and compound is pneumatically loaded into the extruding machines. Much of the noisy machinery has been moved off the production floor, which is clean, well-lighted, and quiet.

The new, reliable technology and quest for standardization have generally been greeted with relief by operators who no longer must "fight the machine" to run an order. One supervisor noted that this produces a new challenge, however. The operators participate in the exciting work of establishing process control, but then the solutions become standardized and running the machine is routinized. "This is a small shop. If they [operators] think only their output is in footage, rather than recognizing working on the teams, they'll stagnate and feel bored."

Computer use is more prominent in NewSite than in Calhoun Wire and Cable. The PRODCON terminals are used by operators, all of whom issue materials to their orders. The extruding machines incorporate computerized control panels and digital displays of run conditions, and operators use computers to type the minutes of meetings, compose memos, and create charts and diagrams. The ubiquitous forms we saw used in Chapter 6 have been greatly condensed, and new ones can be created instantly on the computer.

Operators agreed that both the accuracy and use of information have increased in NewSite. As a result of condensing documents and shortening the "paper trail," operators said they placed more trust in the data they received and did not need to verify so much. Indeed, the efficiency of the new plant reveals how much time was previously devoted to mitigating the effects of errors in paperwork. Improving the production process, however, is predicated on the collection, manipulation, and interpretation of data. Thus, the nature, if not the extent, of the operators' information processing has changed.

These changes in production-floor organization and technology have numerous and subtle effects on work. NewSite's size and its clean and tranquil ambience are most notable. The small size, single product line, and cross-training make face-to-face interactions ubiquitous so that grudges are harder to hold. The cleanliness and JIT philosophy eliminate most hiding places for orders, and they make it easier to diagnose problems. While formal meetings and their permanent records continue to be important, discussions at the location of a problem are now common since the level of noise is greatly reduced. What has declined is the oral tradition of "old wive's tales," as one operator remarked.

The scale of the plant and the commitment to process improvement have also improved feedback, albeit in complex ways. By producing only a single product line under standard conditions there are more opportunities to repeat processes and to learn from outcomes. The small size also facilitates rapid feedback, as does the JIT philosophy. Operators concurred that problems can be solved in weeks or months rather than years.

Still, many of the old problems persist. An extruding operator told of producing some wire and later seeing it being scrapped by someone from another area. He agreed that it was lumpy but was concerned that he had not been informed so he could correct the problem. Of deeper concern to supervisors is that while operators identify problems, the process of assessing them and devising solutions is usually circuitous and time-consuming, and the operators may not link the information they provide with the ultimate action taken. One supervisor reflected that in the old plant operators acted on machines and saw the results immediately. Today, providing feedback on a process eliminates the former "gratification loop." The pacing of work, too, has reduced the time available to receive information. The machine set-ups performed during a shift by Extruding area operators, for example, have increased two-and-a-half times due to the number of small orders and stringent deadlines. Time to contemplate information is often lacking.

Operators, supervisors, and engineers agreed that the plant is greatly improved and better integrated, but tensions persist and new ones have arisen. While disputes between areas are reduced, many of the sentiments that previously characterized them have been transferred to relationships between the shifts. Day shift retains its traditional access to support services and most decisions are made on it. However, the mandates for participation, consensus, and standardization are not realized without full involvement by swing shift, a challenge not always met. The tighter machine scheduling, too, can exacerbate conflict since operators may not have time to prepare machines for the next shift.

The tension between Extruding area operators and other areas persists. The former are classified at higher pay levels and are generally senior, and many retain their faith in the greater skill of their work. Most view extruding as a craft that takes years to learn, and they dislike the cross-training that takes them from their area and brings novices to it.

Junior operators are concentrated in the other areas and many profess to be bored if they remain too long in one area. Most of them support cross-training, and occasions for training are sometimes contentious as senior operators are taught by their juniors.

The voluntary nature of team participation also creates uncertainty about what is valued in the plant. Jose, a marking machine operator, described the three categories of operators he sees in the plant. He, like some others, has joined several teams, trained operators from other areas, and has been cross-trained in several areas. Others have assumed leadership roles on teams but have not been extensively cross-trained. Other operators avoid both the teams and the cross-training. Jose explained that he and his team leader planned to compare pay raises to determine whether leadership, cross-training, or continued mastery of one area is more valued. If operators opting for the last continue to be paid comparably with the others, he asked, why should he move around the plant or assume a leadership role?

The simultaneous commitment to process standardization and JIT manufacturing principles also creates a tension: competition for scarce time in the workplace (Klein 1989). Standardization requires meetings and experiments, and time for these is usually taken from organizational slack. However, slack vanishes as materials flow smoothly between processing steps in an ideally organized JIT environment. Workers are torn between adhering to the JIT pacing or participating in meetings, both of which are formally valued by management.

Finally, there is a continuing and complex tension between the expectations of management and the operator's desire for involvement in the workplace. Supervisors claimed that not only have they improved the workplace and the production process, but they are also providing operators with a more valuable bundle of skills. These are useful not just in NewSite or Calhoun but in other workplaces as well. They realize, however, that some operators do not value their new competencies and others resent the increased demands of their jobs. One denizen of NewSite commented that supervisors and engineers expect the operators to take improvement of the process as seriously as they do, but it is just not as important to many of them. They have been paid well for less demanding work and do not recognize threats to Calhoun's viability. After all, many still see themselves as "short-termers" who will soon be gone.

Working in NewSite thus changes not just skills, but the identity of the individual as a worker and his or her relationship to the workplace. A supervisor explained, "We want to give you another set of skills. Make you as important here as you want to be. Some guys don't want it." Supervisors universally judged the new set of skills to be higher and more transferable, and they felt that operators who failed to develop them and who departed would fail to find better paying jobs. "Most will wind up pumping gas," one concluded.

SKILLS AND WORKPLACES

Our journeys to Kramden Computers and Calhoun Wire and Cable—with a brief stop in NewSite—has revealed a world of work far richer than the one captured in the concept of skill requirements. The latter is widely used to describe the work, but something important is missing from those descriptions. Recovering that which is left out is precisely what is necessary for improving workplaces, as well as workers. We briefly discuss the implications of our journey for each tenet in turn.

First, by decomposing workers and jobs into bundles of skills, abilities, or competencies a sort of composite worker is postulated. Such a fictional character may be useful for some purposes, but we found workplaces populated with real individuals who have idiosyncratic ways of performing nominally identical tasks. It may well be comforting to think in terms of composite workers since to do so is to simplify the tasks of management. We have seen, however, that this individuality not only is a cost but may also bring important benefits to the workplace.

A recurring challenge for each workplace is to distinguish common tasks that must be performed in nearly identical ways, from domains where idiosyncratic styles can be tolerated and may even be an asset. NewSite provides an important lesson here: As performance of many tasks has been standardized, individuals colonized particular aspects of process improvement, bringing their unique talents to bear. Here management's main challenge is simultaneously to gain consensus about what is common and to motivate diversely interested and talented operators to turn their attention to the production process.

Also missing from a focus on discrete skills is the relationship of the workplace to individual identity. The sites we visited were diverse, but calls for worker participation and commitment were strident in each. Participation and commitment may well change job tasks and roles in significant ways, but more important, they represent the penetration of individual identity by organizational actors. Even when NewSite adopted a strategy of offering its operators an improved bundle of skills, many operators demurred, and all set a limit on the "seriousness" with which they would take improving the process.

Second, the notion of requirements proved to be simplistic. Much effort in Calhoun, for example, was devoted to coaxing machines into producing "in spec" wire and cable, and so the ability to do so was clearly necessary. Yet NewSite vividly demonstrates that decades of such requirements may vanish with the purchase of reliable equipment and the provision of accurate information.

We also saw that different categories of people such as managers, engineers, and operators may see different skills as required. Some skills may even be invisible to those who, from the perspective of an outside observer, routinely demonstrate them. The very definition of work in fact is often contentious, much less what is required to perform it.

An important lesson that NewSite teaches is that what is required of the workplace need not be required of each individual within it: The community of practice will likely have capabilities missing in its individual members. By focusing on the presumed common characteristics of individual jobs and by ignoring the community of practice, the concept of skill requirements obscures both the variability in individual performances and the contributions they make to the overall capability of the workplace.

Third, context repeatedly proved to be important. The specific features of particular technologies and forms of organization affect learning in the workplace, and successful workers devise performances that are sensitive to them. Moreover, the local effects of external factors such as technological innovation and global competition are far from inexorable: Managerial choice performs a central role in how they play out. Nor was context external to skill, for workers contributed to developing the workplaces in which they toiled. From Kramden's repair technicians with their stashes of spare parts and the assemblers with their surreptitious documentation, to NewSite's operators who are formally charged with improving the manufacturing process, members of the community of practice work in and on their workplaces.

Fourth, skill failed to provide a neutral description of human activity. What is recognized as skill varies, and the capacity to define a skill is an act of enormous power. The entire edifice of skill requirements typically directs attention to the shortcomings of lower-status workers and away from higher-status managers or engineers. By identifying what is required of workers, it may absolve management of responsibility for providing workplaces in which learning is fostered. Yet NewSite provides testimony to the continuing importance of motivation in the workplace.

The relationships of power that the concept of skill requirements reflects and enacts are especially salient at a time when the corporation's commitment to employees is increasingly tenuous. From this perspective, the supposed "skills gap" appears quite different. Rather than remaining deficient in existing skills, workers may be asked to develop more extensive abilities such as communication and interaction skills, and even to become committed workers in the absence of incentives to do so. The protean worker able to carry a bundle of skills from job to job can thus dampen the effects of workplaces that fail to support learning or to provide incentives for commitment. From this perspective, the "skills gap" may in fact be a "workplace gap."

We need not substitute a list of "learning requirements" for the concept of skill requirements that we have critiqued. Based on our journey, however, we can sketch some of the features that seem to facilitate learning in the workplace. Most of these are quite obvious and unsurprising, but our journey suggests their absence may be significant.

We repeatedly saw that workplaces engage the attention of workers in different ways, and that this structuring of attention underlies learning. The sites we explored differed, sometimes dramatically, in how they directed the worker's attention. We saw that attention can vary spatially as when areas are defined as off-limits or when workers have little reason to explore the workplace in the course of performing their tasks. Alternatively, workers may be encouraged to explore their surroundings. We also saw that attention may be temporally structured, as when workers pay attention to events that can occur weeks or months in the future, or when the duration of their shift is their only concern. The structuring of attention by function is particularly striking when workers do or do not pay attention to larger systems within the workplace.

The structuring of attention does not occur independently of the incentives—and disincentives—to look and act. Workers assess what is rewarded and punished, and what performances count as evidence of good or bad behavior. Incentives and disincentives to look and act are profoundly shaped by managerial choice, but they remain complex and often ambiguous. For example, some of Kramden's workers try to improve manufacturing because of their occupational socialization, and they are explicit that they are acting in spite of management's incompetence. Others, such as the assembler who prepares contraband documentation, are motivated by loyalty to their coworkers. Still others simply enjoy the game of outwitting supervisors and getting away with prohibited acts.

Workers' interpretations and assessments of incentives and disincentives are fundamental. These are embedded in their daily performance of work and are not determined directly by managerial fiat, such as Kramden's demand that each worker cooperate and serve as a vice president. In analyzing any particular workplace we must consider that a problem defined in terms of missing skills and training may be erroneously diagnosed: Workers may have learned well the lessons taught by the workplace that are necessary for continued employment there. These may be quite different from the lessons formally valued by management.

Other features of the workplace also affect learning. The availability and accuracy of information are important. We may think of these as a sort of "transparency" in which workers can see how the production process works and how the larger workplace itself functions. Information is not always accurate in Calhoun Wire and Cable, but there are no systematic barriers to curious workers who in fact are valued by management. Volumes of documentation are readily accessible, and operators are encouraged to use it and to talk with engineers and technicians. They are encouraged to learn about other areas of the plant and even to work temporarily in administrative positions. Kramden Computers, on the other hand, is the "opaque" workplace structured by physical, functional, and symbolic barriers to learning.

The issue of transparency rests on deeper assumptions about work and the relationship of the worker to the workplace. In Kramden Computers, supervisors and engineers said that production work consists of performing predefined tasks, ideally in the way specified by experts. The information required to perform those tasks, too, is predefined. In Calhoun Wire and Cable, work has a much broader definition and the idea that workers need only minimal information is considered foolhardy.

Opportunity to exercise skills is another obvious but necessary characteristic of the workplace. Workers in both sites are often accused of lacking specific skills, when in fact they have few opportunities to demonstrate them. The ability to plan is exemplary. Kramden's supervisors lamented the teams' inability to plan, but the workers spoke of the supervisors' tendency to override their decisions and the general irrelevance of preparing for the future. Calhoun Wire and Cable provides more opportunities to exercise this ability, but they are unevenly distributed. Extruding area operators may plan efficient sequences of orders, but Marking area operators supposedly lack this ability. The former, however, are allowed to "jump schedule," while the latter simply load the next scheduled order.

Supervisors often attributed characteristics of the job to the people holding it, thereby underestimating the abilities of their workers. Kramden's production floor, for example, has many Vietnamese workers who have given up on contributing ideas to an indifferent management. Supervisors said those workers lack initiative and creativity, although many own small businesses that they hope will eventually support them. Many, too, endured considerable hardship to reach this country, and they often attend local community colleges after work.

Finally, the workplaces structure the feedback systems by which workers learn about the actions they take. An elementary model of a regulatory feedback system is useful here. Feedback rests on the ability to detect relevant conditions about the product and the differing states of the production process. Trustworthy information must be collected, transmitted, and stored. Feedback requires standards to which information is compared and the capacity to select appropriate responses based on that comparison. Finally, the system must implement the selected response and learn from the results of doing so.

A functioning feedback system must regulate itself in order to continue to be adaptive. Important issues here include whether feedback is being provided about states of the environment that affect the production process; whether useful information is being collected, stored, and transmitted; and whether the standards of comparison and the possible responses remain appropriate. In assessing such a feedback system, we may ask whether it permits sufficient regulation for the workplace to remain viable, and we may examine how the tasks of regulation are distributed among people.

Production workers in Kramden Computers receive little feedback about their actions, and many practices of management seem designed to prevent learning and feedback. Access to documentation is restricted, and scant data are collected, stored, or transmitted to production workers. The production manager's bemused assertion that no one knew how computers are built is testimony to the inadequacy of feedback in the plant. The production workers' involvement in feedback is directed only at the proverbial "workmanship problems," and not at all at the process of production.

The situation in Calhoun Wire and Cable is very different due to the complexity of the production process there and the proliferation of products. Operators are explicitly allowed access to information; the ability to collect, store, and transmit it; and leeway in adjusting the process. In striking contrast to Kramden Computers, these workers are able to act upon the workplace, and they are involved in investigating and improving the production process. What they lack is the reel-by-reel feedback to link run conditions to specific outcomes.

We have explored two workplaces in considerable depth, and we must be cautious in drawing lessons from such a limited sample. Other workplaces would undoubtedly teach us additional lessons, but the fundamental one we have learned here would likely remain: We ignore the workplace as an arena that structures learning only at great peril (Hull 1993).[1] The picture of work we have painted here is richer than the concepts of skill requirements and a skills gap indicate, and understanding a world populated by real people in real workplaces is essential if workplaces, jobs, and workers are to be improved. This richer picture of work presents a greater challenge to educators and employers than simply demanding improved worker skills, but it also suggests a more hopeful assessment of the capabilities of ordinary people to improve how they work.

Notes

Chapter 1

1. Kramden Computers and Calhoun Wire and Cable Company are pseud-onyms, as are the names of all individuals.

2. Examples of this literature include National Research Council (1983), National Science Board Commission on Precollege Education in Mathematics, Science, and Technology (1983), Committee on Science, Engineering, and Public Policy (1984), National Academy of Sciences (1984), Carnevale, Gainer, and Meltzer (1988), U.S. Departments of Education and Labor (1988), U.S. Departments of Labor, Education, and Commerce (1988), U.S. Department of Labor (1989, 1991), and National Center on Education and the Economy (1990).

3. A comprehensive review of taxonomies of human skills and abilities is provided by Fleishman and Quaintance (1984).

4. The first three of the tenets are discussed in Darrah (1994).

5. Roberts and Glick (1981) make a similar point in critiquing the use of job characteristics approaches to analyze work and prescribe task design.

Chapter 2

1. The argument developed in this and the next chapter was first presented in Darrah (1995).

2. The Educational Requirements for New Technology and Work Organization Project was conducted at the Stanford University School of Education and supported by the Spencer Foundation. Henry Levin (Stanford University) and Russell Rumberger (University of California, Santa Barbara) directed the project. Michelle Deatrick, Christine Finnan, and Alison Work conducted fieldwork in the other project sites.

3. An overview to business and industrial anthropology is provided by Baba (1986). Review articles of the anthropology of industrial work are provided by Burawoy (1979) and Holzberg and Giovannini (1981).

4. "Understanding systems" is defined by the SCANS Report as: "Knows how social, organizational, and technological systems work and operates effectively within them. Demonstrating competence in understanding systems involves knowing how a system's structures relate to goals; responding to the demands of the system/organization; knowing the right people to ask for information and where to get resources; and functioning within the formal and informal codes of the social/organizational system" (U.S. Department of Labor 1992, 2–6).

CHAPTER 4

1. Chapters 4–8 are based on my doctoral dissertation (Darrah 1990) and a previously published article (Darrah 1991).

2. Department names are capitalized throughout (e.g. Packing Department). Because the term *area* is used informally, it is not capitalized (e.g., Cabling area). Some department and area names have been changed to provide confidentiality.

3. The spelling of some machine parts and tasks is inconsistent in the plant (e.g. "pay off," "payoff," and "pay-off"). The hyphenated variants of "set-up," "put-up," "take-up," and "pay-off" are used throughout.

CHAPTER 7

1. The role of informal lessons and enculturation into organizational or occupational worldviews is typical of ethnographic studies of work. See, for example, Gamst (1980), Applebaum (1981), Agar (1986), and Wellman (1986).

2. The concept of organizational worldview is closely related to that of organizational culture. The latter can be distinguished from corporate culture which is typically created and manipulated by management for strategic purposes. The former may emerge from the experiences of people working in an organization or one of its subunits. Articles by Baba, Gamst, Hamada, Jordan, and Michaelson in a 1989 special issue of the *Anthropology of Work Review* ("Anthropological Approaches to Organizational Culture") provide an excellent discussion of the issues. The concepts of organizational and corporate culture are used by scholars and practitioners in other disciplines and fields, contributing to the variety of definitions.

CHAPTER 9

1. These characteristics are also broadly complementary to Knowles' theory of adult learning (Knowles 1984). This theory conceptualizes adult learning as deeply embedded in a person's life, and does not isolate learning in classrooms. It assumes that the learning of adults is shaped by their need to know, their self-concept and experiences, their readiness and orientation to learn, and their motivation to do so.

REFERENCES

Adler, Paul. 1986. New technologies, new skills. *California Management Review* 29(1): 9–28.

Agar, Michael. 1986. *Independents Declared: The Dilemmas of Independent Trucking.* Washington, DC: Smithsonian Institution Press.

Applebaum, Herbert. 1981. *Royal Blue: The Culture of Construction Workers.* San Francisco: Holt, Rinehart & Winston.

Attewell, Paul. 1987. The deskilling controversy. *Work and Occupations* 14(3): 323–346.

Baba, Marietta. 1986. *Business and Industrial Anthropology: An Overview* (NAPA Bulletin 2). Washington, DC: National Association for the Practice of Anthropology, American Anthropological Association.

———. 1991. The skill requirements of work: An ethnographic approach. *Anthropology of Work Review* 12(3): 2–11.

Balfanz, Robert. 1990. Elementary school quality, the mathematics curriculum, and the role of local knowledge. *International Review of Education* 36(1): 43–56.

Becker, Gary. 1975. *Human Capital.* 2d ed. New York: Columbia University Press.

Bernstein, Richard. 1976. *The Restructuring of Social and Political Theory.* New York: Harcourt Brace Jovanovich.

Blauner, Robert. 1964. *Alienation and Freedom: The Factory Worker and His Industry.* Chicago: University of Chicago Press.

Bourdieu, Pierre. 1977. *Outline of a Theory of Practice.* New York: Cambridge University Press.

Braverman, Harry. 1974. *Labor and Monopoly Capitalism.* New York: Monthly Review Press.

Brown, John Seely, Allan Collins, and Paul Duguid. 1989. Situated cognition and the culture of learning. *Educational Researcher* (January–February): 32–42.

Burawoy, Michael. 1979. The anthropology of industrial work. In *Annual Review of Anthropology,* 231–266. Palo Alto, CA: Annual Reviews.

Carnevale, Anthony, Leila Gainer, and Ann Meltzer. 1988. *Workplace Basics: The Basic Skills Employers Want.* Alexandria, VA: American Society for Training and Development/U.S. Department of Labor.

Cockburn, Cynthia. 1985. *Machinery of Dominance.* Dover, NH: Pluto Press.

Collins, Randall. 1979. *The Credential Society.* New York: Academic Press.

Committee on Science, Engineering, and Public Policy. 1984. *High Schools and the Changing Workplace: The Employer's View.* Report of the Panel on Secondary School Education for the Changing Workplace, Committee on Science, Engineering, and Public Policy. Washington, DC: National Academy Press.

Cornfield, Dan. 1987. *Workers, Managers, and Technological Change.* New York: Plenum.

Cyert, Richard, and David Mowery. 1989. Technology, employment, and U.S. competitiveness. *Scientific American* 260(5): 54–62.

Darrah, Charles. 1990. Skills in context: An exploration in industrial ethnography. Ph.D. diss., School of Education, Stanford University.

———. 1991. Workplace skills in context. *Human Organization* 51: 264–273.

———. 1994. Skill requirements at work: Rhetoric versus reality. *Work and Occupations* 21(1): 64–84.

———. 1995. Workplace training, workplace learning. *Human Organization* 54: 31–41.

Deal, Terrence, and Allen Kennedy. 1982. *Corporate Cultures: The Rites and Rituals of Corporate Life.* Menlo Park, CA: Addison-Wesley.

Diehl, William and Larry Mikulecky. 1980. The nature of reading at work. *Journal of Reading* (December): 221–227.

Engestrom, Yrjo. 1987. *Learning by Expanding: An Activity-Theoretical Approach to Developmental Research.* Helsinki: Orienta-Konsultit Oy.

Fleishman, Edwin. 1975. Toward a taxonomy of human performance. *Human Performance* 30(12): 1127–1149.

Fleishman, Edwin, and Marilyn Quaintance. 1984. *Taxonomies of Human Performance.* San Francisco: Academic Press.

Form, William. 1987. On the degradation of skills. *Annual Review of Sociology* 13: 29–47.

Gamst, Frederick. 1980. *The Hoghead.* San Francisco: Holt, Rinehart & Winston.

Gartman, David. 1986. *Auto Slavery: The Labor Process in the American Automobile Industry, 1897–1950.* New Brunswick, NJ: Rutgers University Press.

Geertz, Clifford. 1973. *The Interpretation of Cultures.* New York: Basic Books.

Giddens, Anthony. 1979. *Central Problems in Social Theory.* Berkeley, CA: University of California Press.

Goodman, Paul, Terri Griffith, and Deborah Fenner. 1990. Understanding technology and the individual in an organizational context. In *Technology and Organizations,* Paul Goodman, Lee Sproull, and Associates, eds. San Francisco: Jossey-Bass.

Goodnow, Jaqueline. 1980. Differences in popular theories of instruction. In *Cognition, Development, and Instruction,* John Kirby and John Briggs, eds., 187–197. New York: Academic Press.

Greeno, Joseph. 1988a. *Situations, Mental Models, and Generative Knowledge.* IRL Report 88-0005. Palo Alto, CA: Institute for Research on Learning.

———. 1988b. *A Perspective on Thinking.* IRL Report 88-0010. Palo Alto, CA: Institute for Research on Learning.

Gruenfeld, Elaine. 1981. *Performance Appraisal: Promise and Peril.* Ithaca, NY: New York State School of Industrial and Labor Relations, Cornell University.

Hackman, Richard, and Greg Oldham. 1980. *Work Redesign.* Menlo Park, CA: Addison-Wesley.

Halle, David. 1984. *America's Working Man.* Chicago: University of Chicago Press.

Henderson, Richard. 1980. *Practical Guide to Performance Appraisal.* Reston, VA: Reston Publishing.

Hirschhorn, Larry. 1984. *Beyond Mechanization.* Cambridge, MA: MIT Press.

Hochschild, Arlie. 1983. *The Managed Heart: Commercialization of Human Feeling.* Berkeley, CA: University of California Press.

Holzberg, Carol, and Maureen Giovannini. 1981. Anthropology and industry: Reappraisal and new directions. In *Annual Review of Anthropology,* 317–360. Palo Alto, CA: Annual Reviews.

Hull, Glynda. 1993. Hearing other voices: A critical assessment of popular views on literacy and work. *Harvard Educational Review* 63(1): 20–49.

Jacob, Evelyn. 1986. Literacy skills and production line work. In *Becoming a Worker,* Kathryn Borman and Jane Reisman, eds., 176–200. Norwood, NJ: Ablex.

Juravich, Tom. 1985. *Chaos on the Shopfloor: A Worker's View of Quality, Produc-*

tivity, and Management. Philadelphia: Temple University Press.

Kearney, Michael. 1984. *World View*. Novato, CA: Chandler and Sharp.

Kelley, Maryellen. 1990. New process technology, job design, and work organization: A contingency model. *American Sociological Review* 55: 191–208.

Klein, Janice. 1989. The human cost of manufacturing reform. *Harvard Business Review* 67(2): 60–64.

Knowles, Malcolm. 1984. *The Adult Learner: A Neglected Species*. 3rd ed. Houston: Gulf Publishing Company.

Kraft, Philip. 1979. The industrialization of computer programming: From programming to "software production." In *Case Studies on the Labor Process*, Andrew Zimbalist, ed., 1–17. New York: Monthly Review Press.

Kunda, Gideon. 1992. *Engineering Culture: Control and Commitment in a High-Tech Corporation*. Philadelphia: Temple University Press.

Kusterer, Ken. 1978. *Know-How on the Job: The Important Working Knowledge of "Unskilled" Workers*. Boulder, CO: Westview Press.

Lave, Jean. 1988. *Cognition in Practice*. New York: Cambridge University Press.

Lave, Jean, and Etienne Wenger. 1991. *Situated Learning: Legitimate Peripheral Participation*. New York: Cambridge University Press.

McCormick, Ernest. 1979. *Job Analysis: Methods and Applications*. New York: AMACOM.

Meyer, John, and Brian Rowan. 1977. Institutionalized organizations: Formal structure as myth and ceremony. *American Journal of Sociology* 83(2): 340–363.

National Academy of Sciences. 1984. *High Schools and the Changing Workplace: The Employer's View*. Washington, DC: National Academy Press.

National Center on Education and the Economy. 1990. *America's Choice: High Skills or Low Wages!* Report of the Commission on the Skills of the American Workforce. Rochester, NY: Author.

National Commission on Excellence in Education. 1983. *A Nation at Risk*. Washington, DC: U.S. Government Printing Office.

National Research Council. 1983. *Education for Tomorrow's Jobs*. Committee on Vocational Education and Economic Development in Depressed Areas. Washington, DC: National Academy Press.

National Science Board Commission on Precollege Education in Mathematics, Science and Technology. 1983. *Educating Americans for the 21st Century*. Washington, DC: National Science Foundation.

Neisser, Ulric. 1983. Toward a skillful psychology. In *The Acquisition of Symbolic Skills*. Donald Rogers and John Sloboda, eds., 1–17. New York: Plenum.

Noble, David. 1984. *Forces of Production*. New York: Alfred Knopf.

Norton, Robert. 1985. *DACUM Handbook*. Columbus: Ohio State University, National Center for Research in Vocational Education.

Orr, Julian. 1990. Talking about machines: An ethnography of a modern job. Ph.D. diss., Cornell University.

———. 1991. Contested knowledge. *Anthropology of Work Review* 12(3): 12–17.

Ortner, Sherry. 1984. *Theory in anthropology since the sixties*. Society for Comparative Study of Society and History, 126–166.

Peters, Thomas, and Robert Waterman. 1982. *In Search of Excellence*. New York: Harper & Row.

Raizen, Senta. 1989. *Reforming Education for Work: A Cognitive Science Perspective*. Berkeley, CA: National Center for Research in Vocational Education.

Reskin, Barbara, and Patricia Roos. 1990. *Job Queues, Gender Queues: Explaining Women's Inroads into Male Occupations*. Philadelphia: Temple University Press.

Resnick, Lauren, John Levine, and Stephanie Teasley. 1991. *Perspectives on Socially Shared Cognition*. Washington, DC: American Psychological Association.

Roberts, Karlene, and William Glick. 1981. The job characteristics approach to task design: A critical review. *Journal of Applied Psychology* 66(2): 193–217.

Saxe, Geoffrey. 1988. Candy selling and math learning. *Educational Researcher* (August–September): 14–21.

Scribner, Sylvia. 1984. Studying working intelligence. In *Everyday Cognition: Its Development in Social Context,* Barbara Rogoff and Jean Lave, eds., 9–40. Cambridge, MA: Harvard University Press.

———. 1986. Thinking in action: Some characteristics of practical thought. In *Practical Intelligence.* Robert Sternberg and Richard Wagner, eds., 13–30. New York: Cambridge University Press.

———. 1992. Mind in action: A functional approach to thinking. Invited address, 1983 biennial meeting of the Society for Research in Child Development. *Quarterly Newsletter of the Laboratory of Comparative Human Cognition* 14(4): 103–110.

Special issue: Anthropological approaches to organizational culture. *Anthropology of Work Review* 10(3): 1–19, 1989.

Spenner, Kenneth. 1979. Temporal changes in work content. *American Sociological Review* 44: 746–762.

———. 1983. Deciphering Prometheus: Temporal change in the skill level of work. *American Sociological Review* 48: 824–837.

———. 1988. Technological change, skill requirements, and education: The case for uncertainty. In *The Impact of Technological Change on Employment and Economic Growth,* Richard Cyert and David Mowery, eds., 131–184. Cambridge, MA: Ballinger.

———. 1990. Skill: Meaning, methods, and measures. *Work and Occupations* 17(4): 399–421.

Sternberg, Robert, and David Caruso. 1985. Practical modes of knowing. In *Learning and Teaching the Ways of Knowing,* Elliot Eisner, ed., 133–158. Chicago: University of Chicago Press.

Sternberg, Robert, and Richard Wagner. 1986. *Practical Intelligence: Nature and Origins of Competence in the Everyday World.* New York: Cambridge University Press.

Suchman, Lucy. 1987. *Plans and Situated Actions: The Problem of Human-Machine Communication.* New York: Cambridge University Press.

Thomas, Robert. 1994. *What Machines Can't Do.* Berkeley, CA: University of California Press.

Thompson, Paul. 1983. *The Nature of Work.* London: Macmillan.

U.S. Department of Labor. 1977. *Dictionary of Occupational Titles.* 4th ed. Washington, DC: U.S. Government Printing Office.

———. 1989. *Investing in People: A Strategy to Address America's Workforce Crisis.* Washington, DC: U.S. Government Printing Office.

———. 1991. *What Work Requires of Schools* (SCANS Report). Washington, DC: U.S. Government Printing Office.

———. 1992. *Skills and Tasks for Jobs* (SCANS Report). Washington, DC: U.S. Government Printing Office.

U.S. Departments of Education and Labor. 1988. *The Bottom Line: Basic Skills in the Workplace.* Washington, DC: U.S. Government Printing Office.

U.S. Departments of Labor, Education, and Commerce. 1988. *Building a Quality Workforce.* Washington, DC: U.S. Government Printing Office.

Vallas, Steven. 1988. New technology, job content, and worker alienation: A test of two rival perspectives. *Work and Occupations* 15: 148–178.

———. 1990. The concept of skill: A critical review. *Work and Occupations* 17(4): 379–398.

Vygotsky, Lev. 1978. *Mind in Society: The Development of Higher Psychological Processes.* Cambridge, MA: Harvard University Press.

———. 1986. *Thought and Language.* Cambridge, MA: MIT Press.

Wallace, Michael, and Arne Kalleberg. 1982. Industrial transformation and decline of craft: The decomposition of skill in the printing industry. *American Sociological Review* 47: 307–324.

Wellman, David. 1986. Learning at work: The etiquette of longshoring. In *Becoming a Worker,* Kathryn Borman and Jane Reisman, eds., 176–200. Norwood, NJ: Ablex.

Wertsch, James. 1985. *Culture, Communication, and Cognition: Vygotskian Perspectives.* New York: Cambridge University Press.

Wilkinson, Barry. 1983. *The Shopfloor Politics of New Technology.* London: Heineman Educational Books.

Zimbalist, Andrew. 1979. *Case Studies on the Labor Process.* New York: Monthly Review Press.

Zuboff, Shoshana. 1988. *In the Age of the Smart Machine.* New York: Basic Books.

INDEX

compound, 76, 78–79, 123, 128
"control by ignorance," 19, 25, 33,
cooperation, 32–33, 97, 126
Cornfield, Dan, 7
cross-training, 38, 121, 153, 155, 162, 166
Customer Service Department, 28
"cutting on the fly," 75
Cyert, Richard, 8

DACUM, 10
"dancer," 59, 61
data entry, 96, 97, 99–101, 150
Deal, Terrence, 26
Dean, 15, 19, 20, 24, 35
"deep acting," 26
Department 1000, 56
    grand tour of, 57–60
Department 2000, 56
Department 3000, 56
Design Engineering Department, 32
"deskilling," 147
Dictionary of Occupational Titles, 8, 9–10,
Diehl, William, 48
"dinging," 124–125
documentation, 37, 42–43, 98–105, 164–
    165
"downtime," 100, 129
Doyle, 142–143, 145–146, 147
Duguid, Paul, 48
Dwight, 122

Eddie, 120–121
Edward, 3–4
efficiency, 128–129
electrotrude tooling, 109–110, 111
Elmore, 128
enculturation, 14, 129
Engestrom, Yrjo, 46
Eric, 65–66, 67
errors, 153
ethnicity, 131
Extruding Area, 56, 57–59, 73, 74–81, 99,
    108, 112, 115, 119, 123, 127, 129,
    130, 131, 133, 135, 163, 165, 166,
    171
    characteristics of, 80–81
    cleanouts, 76
    data entry, 58–59, 75–76, 78
    Extruder 40, 60
    inspection, 75–76
    machines, 60–62, 107
    monitoring, 79–80
    paperwork, 74–75
    procedures, 65
    running machines, 60–62, 74–81

setting-up, 76–78, 165
troubleshooting, 80–81

family, metaphor of, 131
faulty wire, 80, 89–90, 98, 99, 101
Federico, 91
feedback, 165, 171
"feel," 84
Fenner, Deborah, 7
fieldwork, 16, 17, 55, 124, 126, 139
Fleishman, Edwin, 9
flowcharts, 163–164
Form, William, 7
Fred, 143, 145–147
future workplace skills literature, 5–6

Gainer, Leila, 12
Gartman, David, 7
GEECO, 65
Geertz, Clifford, 6
gender, 131–132
Giddens, Anthony, 46
Goodman, Paul, 7
Goodnow, Jaqueline, 36
"good worker," 115–117, 155, 158
"grabbing gravy," 162
grand tours, 57–60
Greeno, Joseph, 46
Griffith, Terri, 7
Gruenfeld, Elaine, 10

Hackman, Richard, 10
Halle, David, 9
helping, 126–127
Henderson, Richard, 10
hiring, 17–18, 115, 133
Hirschhorn, Larry, 7, 9
Hochschild, Arlie, 26, 27
Homer, 57–60, 65, 67, 130
Hull, Glynda, 172
Human Resources Department, 17, 55

identity, 27, 141, 149, 153–154, 167, 168
incentives, 4, 27, 38–39, 96, 125, 137, 169–
    170
individualism, 129–131, 140, 154, 158
"in-spec," 80–81
instruction, 38–39, 40–41
    popular theories of, 36
interruptions, 20, 31
Ivan, 102–103

Jacob, Evelyn, 48
Japanese manufacturers, 96
Jason, 91